NEW COMPLETE
DOG TRAINING
MANUAL

NEW COMPLETE
DOG TRAINING
MANUAL

DR. BRUCE FOGLE

with PATRICIA HOLDEN WHITE

LONDON, NEW YORK, MUNICH,
MELBOURNE, DELHI

A PENGUIN COMPANY

Senior Editor **Heather Jones**
Senior Art Editor **Wendy Bartlet**
Managing Editor **Deirdre Headon**
Managing Art Editor **Lee Griffiths**
Art Director **Carole Ash**
DTP Designer **Louise Waller**
Production Controller **Mandy Inness**
Picture Research **Samantha Nunn**
Dog Training Consultant **Patricia Holden White**

Edited by **Sands Publishing Solutions** (Editorial Department)
7 Harringay Gardens, London N8 0SE

Design assistance: **Lovelock & Co.**
The Basement, 31 Montpelier Street, Brighton BN1 3DL

RSPCA Trading Limited (which covenants all its taxable profits to the RSPCA,
Registered Charity No. 219099) receives a royalty for every copy of this book sold by
Dorling Kindersley and will receive a minimum of £500 from the sale of this book. Details
of royalties payable to RSPCA Trading Limited can be obtained by writing to the Publisher,
Dorling Kindersley Limited at 80 Strand, London WC2R 0RL. For the purposes of the
Charities Act 1992, no further seller of this book shall be deemed to be a commercial
participator with the RSPCA. RSPCA name and logo are trademarks of the RSPCA
used by Dorling Kindersley under license from RSPCA Trading Limited.

First published in Great Britain in 1994 as *Complete Dog Training Manual*
by Dorling Kindersley Limited, 80 Strand, London WC2R 0RL

2 4 6 8 10 9 7 5 3

A CIP catalogue record for this book
is available from the British Library.

ISBN 0-7513-3867-2

Colour reproduced by Colourscan, Singapore

Printed and bound in Spain by Artes Gráficas Toledo, S.A.U
D.L.TO:1015-2002

For our complete catalogue visit

www.dk.com

Contents

Introduction

Some of you know I'm a practising veterinarian, not a professional dog trainer. When I was starting out, I learned early on how important good dog behaviour is: it makes or breaks relationships between us and our canine buddies. I quickly realized that answering questions about behaviour and training was just as important as answering those about health and welfare.

Patricia Holden White, also urban-bred and a lifelong dog owner, is both a literary agent and a professional dog trainer.

We hope you find the training we share with you in this book enjoyable for you and your dog. It's simple and logical – just remember you are training a wolf in disguise, not a quasi-human.

There are a few easy rules about dog training: keep it short, keep it simple, keep it fun – for both of you. Your attitude and freshness during training is as important as your dog's. If you're not in the mood, forget it – postpone until you are. Your objective is to reinforce the social relationship your dog should have with you. You are leader of the pack and your dog is an obedient follower.

The dog evolved from the wolf and has lived with humans for over 10,000 years. By 6,000 years ago, dogs had been bred with the looks, sizes, and abilities we still see today.

In all regions of the northern hemisphere, people formed constructive relationships with dogs, and generations of selective breeding resulted in dogs becoming specialized in their abilities to work for and with humans.

By the end of the 19th century, over 400 breeds of dogs were recognized by kennel clubs around the world. Virtually all of these breeds exist today, but the dog's role is still evolving. Today, most dogs are bred for companionship, and this can create problems.

For thousands of years, dogs were asked to use their mental and physical abilities. Modern dogs may be healthier and protected from danger in our luxurious homes, but many lead boring lives, and this can lead to behavioural problems.

Rescue-centre statistics show that the dogs most likely to be "given up" are under two years old with behavioural problems. In some parts of the world the most common cause of death in dogs under two years old is euthanasia because of such problems.

All this is avoidable. Dog training is simple as long as you understand and enjoy what you are doing. In a complicated world it's wonderful to have the uncomplicated companionship of a well-trained dog. With this book, that is yours for the taking.

Your Dog's Mind

Dogs share a range of needs, feelings, and emotions with people. They are sociable and thrive on companionship, with their own kind and with us. They enjoy mental and physical exercise. They respond to rewards and develop bad habits when bored. They are always learning, not just when they are being schooled. However, dogs are not people in disguise. Each dog has its own personality, intelligence, tolerance, and trainability. Despite centuries of selective breeding, your dog still thinks like its wolf ancestors. It is a pack animal wanting to know its place in the pack and respond to the pack leader's commands. In your dog's mind you and your family are pack leaders. You make decisions and your dog complies. Understand how your dog thinks and training will be enjoyable for both of you.

Breed Differences

Humans have been breeding dogs for at least 10,000 years. Dogs were originally bred for behaviour and ability, such as hunting, herding, and guarding but in the last 200 years they have been bred primarily for their size, coat, and colour. Specific breeds are associated with certain aspects of behaviour, and some types of dog are better predisposed towards training than others.

Gun dogs

Dogs such as Weimaraners, Labrador retrievers, setters, and springers love their work. Even as pets, they should work to satisfy their need to please and contain their energy.

Scent hounds

Bloodhounds, basset hounds, and beagles were bred to follow scent, work in packs, and howl signals to their masters. They communicate well with other dogs, and are able to follow even the weakest trails.

Herding breeds

German shepherds, collies, and cattle dogs were evolved to work with farmers and shepherds. Originally bred for stamina and to nip at the heels of livestock, they are loyal and energetic.

Additional information

Sex differences

In the same way that different breeds of dog have certain personality profiles, the different sexes have traits peculiar to them. The male dog's brain is "masculinized" by a surge of male hormones just before it is born. That is why, even before puberty, males tend to grow bigger and behave in the classically masculine ways of being territorial and dominant. At puberty, and again at around two years of age, the behaviour of male dogs can become exaggerated – often making training difficult. The female dog's brain, however, is "neutral" at birth and becomes "feminized" at puberty. Female hormones produced at this stage in the dog's life can increase possessive behaviour and can alter mood, change taste buds, and increase the dog's need to den. Neutering just before sexual maturity often guarantees that your dog's existing personality will be maintained.

Working dogs

Be it guarding (boxers) or sledding (malamutes) these dogs were bred to do a specific job. They need both mental and physical exercise.

Utility dogs

Most of the breeds in this group, like poodles and Dalmatians, are more likely to be kept as pets than used in their original working capacity.

Terriers

Developed to chase small game and vermin, most terriers are small, robust diggers with powerful barks. They rarely back down when challenged.

Toy dogs

Dogs such as chihuahuas, Cavalier King Charles spaniels, Yorkshire terriers, and bichons were bred for companionship and thrive on human contact.

Personality Types

Although each breed of dog has its own personality profile, ultimately every dog is unique. While some dogs are extroverts and like to be the centre of attention, others are more submissive. Both types of dog can be well trained, but different approaches are needed. Where your dog has come from and what it has experienced early in life will also affect its ability to be trained.

Co-operative dog responds enthusiastically to training

Dominant dog resists owner's commands

Co-operative and responsive

The dogs that are easiest to train are those that have a natural curiosity coupled with an affinity with humans. Dogs that investigate and listen to people respond more quickly to training than submissive, fearful dogs or exceedingly dominant individuals.

Dominant and confident

Some dogs, regardless of breed, have naturally confident personalities. The dog's gender also affects its trainability. Neutered dogs and females between seasons are easiest to train. Unneutered male dogs tend to be more dominant and confident and, as a result, they can be less responsive.

Personality traits

Compromise

Most dogs are neither submissive nor dominant. In different circumstances and with different individuals, they can be either dominant or submissive. Most dogs have a mixture of both behaviours in their personalities.

Manipulation

Some dogs dominate their owners by claiming to be submissive. A dog that does this may scratch at its owner's legs and demand to be picked up, for example. These dogs have learned different methods of showing authority.

Submission

Intensely submissive dogs avoid eye contact, tuck their tails between their legs, and collapse in fear when anyone approaches them.

Distraction

Some dogs are more interested in playing with other dogs than in obeying their owners. Often, these dogs were not properly socialized with people as puppies. At first, train this type of dog on its own, rather than in a class.

*Dog cowers
fearfully*

Submissive and insecure

Dogs with submissive personalities can be overwhelmed when commanded to obey. These dogs require a slow and gentle approach during training, so you should not issue commands too harshly. If you have never trained a dog before, consider seeking professional help.

Pecking order

A dog must obey all human members of its family. It should learn that in some circumstances – for example, when it hears a noise outside the window – it may express its dominance by barking a warning. In other circumstances, for example when a family member issues a command, it must obey.

Early Learning

A dog's behaviour is influenced by its mother and littermates. For example, if a mother barks to attract attention, her puppies will behave in the same way. A dog's personality develops between three and 12 weeks of age. The best time to acquire a puppy is when it is about eight weeks old. Exposing it to varied experiences during the following month will lay the groundwork for rewarding training.

Puppy learns to play with its own toys

Meeting people

Make sure that the new puppy meets as many people as possible while still very young. With your vet's permission, take the puppy in the car, to work, and to friends' homes whenever possible. Let it play with dogs that you know are healthy, and introduce it to children and other adults.

Personal investigation

Playing with toys will provide your puppy with mental and physical stimulation, and prevent it from becoming destructive. Find out which toys the puppy prefers (making sure that they are unlike other domestic articles) and use them as rewards during training.

Problem solving

Social development

The best time for dogs to learn to behave properly, both with their own species and with others, especially humans, is when they are under four months old. Supervised puppy evenings *(see page 170)* and early socialization to other species reduces the likelihood of future problems. Restricted contact with humans as a puppy can limit the dog's ability to obey commands. Before acquiring a dog, find out all you can about its early experiences.

Give immediate rewards

When the puppy obeys a command, make sure you always offer an immediate reward, such as gentle stroking or soothing words. As the dominant member of the partnership, you should always be in control.

Early habits endure

Do not get your puppy used to being carried constantly when it is very young. If you do, your dog will expect a similar treatment whenever it feels insecure as an adult.

Puppy instinctively knows that it is being dominated

Puppy eagerly takes part in play activity

Understanding fear

Overseeing all the puppy's activities will ensure that frightening situations are kept to a minimum. Whether developed when interacting with dogs, humans or other entities, fears that a dog learns at an early age can become lifelong phobias unless they are rapidly overcome.

Give mental stimulation

If actively stimulated as puppies, dogs become adept at both learning and problem solving. A puppy learns by observing its mother's behaviour. Within a human family, one person should be the "mother's substitute", responsible for training the puppy, although all family members should participate.

Perfect Timing

When you begin training, make sure your dog knows that rewards are at hand. Praise and reward your dog the instant it responds to your commands. Once your dog has learned your word and hand signals, begin to give fewer food rewards. Reprimand your dog only when you actually observe it misbehaving – displaying anger after the event will simply confuse the dog.

"Stay"

"Wait"

"Good dog to come"

Eye contact
Give verbal commands and hand signals when only when you have eye contact with the dog. Do not overstimulate the dog by using too many food rewards. Try to be aware of how many you are giving.

Body language
Anticipate the dog's behaviour by observing its body language. Give commands when you notice that the dog is beginning to lose concentration – not after it disobeys you.

Instant rewards
Reward the dog as soon as it complies with your command. At first, combine food rewards with verbal praise. After a while, give fewer food rewards, but always give either physical or verbal praise.

Common mistakes

Reinforcement

Rewarding the dog intermittently is the most effective way of reinforcing behaviour, but you should only reinforce good behaviour.

Unplanned reward

As a dog chases a bicycle, the cyclist rides away and the dog wrongly receives an instant, satisfying, and well-timed reward. The timing of the reward reinforces the behaviour.

Anticipating behaviour

The moment your dog makes eye contact with another dog, turn its head away to break the eye line. This should be done before the dog raises its hackles, growls, or begins to pull on the lead.

"Leave it"

Firm command

A verbal command, such as "Leave it", together with an unexpected and unpleasant – but harmless – squirt from a water pistol, is an effective way of reprimanding the dog if it misbehaves.

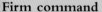

Giving Commands

Dogs respond best to short, sharp commands, given with obvious hand signals. Avoid constantly repeating a command, since this will confuse your dog. Attract your pet's attention by speaking its name, then give your command. The inflection in your voice is important, as are facial expressions. Smile when you are pleased, and scowl at the dog if it wilfully disobeys your command.

"Zen"

"Zen come"

Attracting attention
Use the dog's name to attract its attention. Stand upright, with your shoulders back, and keep the dog's concentration focused on you. As an incentive you might want to show the dog the food reward.

Welcoming body language
Encourage the dog to respond to you by assuming a welcoming posture. Smile, use a friendly and exciting tone of voice, and open your arms to receive the dog. Be generous with your praise.

Additional information

Understanding language

Dogs respond best to short words. Give the dog a one- or two-syllable name, ensuring that it is unlike other common words. Choose a simple word like "Free" or "OK" as the release from a command.

Unintentional approval

If a shy dog backs away from a stranger, and you reassure it by saying "It's OK", you are telling it that you approve of its behaviour. Allow the dog plenty of space and time to accept the stranger naturally.

The value of "No"

The timing of your commands and knowing when to say "No" are important elements of dog training. A "No" should always be followed by a positive command of what you want the dog to do.

Body language

Dogs can read human body language and they will notice when you lose concentration or become bored with the training session. Always try to keep the dog's attention by being alert during training.

"No"

"Zen sit"

Dog learns that owner's right arm raised at elbow means "Sit"

Stern body language

When the dog misbehaves, assume a threatening posture, and look angry when using negative commands. "No" is one of the most important words a dog will learn, since it can prevent it from doing something dangerous. If you have a dog that disobeys you persistently, seek professional advice.

Hand signals

Teach the dog to respond to a combination of spoken and visual commands. When the dog is some distance away from you, you can control it by calling its name and using dramatic hand signals.

Putting it all Together

Training should be enjoyable for both you and your dog. Begin training in a quiet environment, and increase the distractions over several weeks, until the dog behaves well in any environment. Keep the sessions short, only train when you and your dog are alert, and never issue commands you cannot enforce. End each session on a positive note.

"Sit"

Short lessons

Dogs have shorter attention spans than humans. You should train the dog for a maximum of 15 minutes, only twice a day. Do not attempt to train if either you or your dog are finding it difficult to concentrate.

Optimum time

It is best to train when the dog is hungry. It will be mentally alert, and will respond best to food rewards. Giving a dog two meals a day creates time for two good training sessions.

Problem solving

Less potent rewards

Over a few days, reduce the frequency of edible and physical rewards, but always give verbal praise. The dog will soon learn to respond to verbal praise alone.

Training outdoors

Once the dog reliably obeys commands in your home, move to a quiet location outdoors and repeat the training sessions. Make sure you are always in a position of control, so that you are able to enforce your commands.

Primary rewards

Use a selection of treats, rewarding best performances with the tastiest. Dogs which become excessively food-oriented are better trained with toys as a reward.

Training is not exercise

Training is not a substitute for exercise or play time. Ensure that the dog gets the exercise its temperament, breed, and age require.

"Come Lady"

Enforcing commands

Only give commands if you know you are in control. This dog has been distracted but, because it is on a lead, the owner knows she can enforce compliance even if the food lure and verbal command are disregarded.

Finish with fun

Always finish training with something the dog enjoys and is able to do. Play with the dog, but do not save the greatest rewards for the end of the training session. If you do, the dog will want to end the exercise quickly in order to receive its final reward.

Realistic Expectations

Dogs are wonderful. Their ability to hear and especially to smell is far greater than ours. Their strength, tenacity, and endurance has enabled people to inhabit the most inhospitable regions of the world. Dogs readily and willingly want to learn. But there is a problem in our union with dogs and it is our problem. A dog thinks like a dog, not like a human.

Points to consider

Before you get a dog

The whole family needs to be in agreement regarding what sort of dog they want and can cope with. A good dog book like *The New Encyclopedia of the Dog* will help you evaluate the various aspects of owning particular breeds. Your local veterinary nurse should be able to put you in touch with your local dog-training club. Visit them before you get your dog and discuss what owning your chosen breed entails and whether the breed has any inherent health deficiencies. If possible, talk to people who own that breed.

Rehomed dogs

Dogs from shelters and rescue centres usually make wonderful pets. Often the reason they are available for re-homing has a human cause, rather than anything to do with the dog, so find out as much as you can about the dog's background and needs before you make the decision to adopt.

Dogs are not human

The most common mistake I see dog owners make is to expect too much human logic from their canine companion. Your dog may appear almost human in its ability to understand your feelings and emotions, but its natural relationship with other dogs is radically different to our natural relationship with other people. Treat your dog as a valued member of the pack but

never as leader of the pack. Following the do's and don'ts on the opposite page will help get you on track for a realistic relationship with your dog.

Who trains?

One person in the family should be responsible for training the dog, but all members of the family should co-ordinate in the training to remove as much confusion for the dog as possible and to keep the training consistent. Seriously consider joining your local dog-training club, where you will be able to socialize your dog under control and supervision and pick up many useful tips on bringing up your puppy or dog.

Dogs need to be dogs

It is vitally important that dogs meet and socialize with other dogs on a regular basis. Few dogs really thrive in a housebound situation if they are unable to socialize with their own kind.

Consider veterinary insurance

Bills for surgery or long-term illnesses can be enormous and you really need to be aware of this before committing to dog ownership. It can be worth taking out pet insurance just to be on the safe side.

Additional information

Buying a dog

Don't buy a dog for someone else. Don't buy a dog because you feel sorry for it. Don't buy a dog as a knee-jerk reaction. Do it calmly, rationally, and with as much thought and information as possible. Never buy a dog simply because you like what it looks like. All puppies are adorable – but all puppies grow up. If you are not 100 per cent committed to owning a dog, with all its ups and downs, don't do it. A dog really should be for life. Be honest in evaluating why you want a dog. Dogs should not be child or other human-relation substitutes. People who treat dogs as child substitutes often provoke real behaviour problems in their dogs.

DO	DON'T
Be realistic with your expectations.	Treat your dog as a child substitute.
Treat your dog as someone who should implicitly do as it is told.	Apply democratic principles to your relationship with your dog.
Give clear and concise commands.	Implore or use sentences that start "If you do that again...".
Be consistent.	Deviate occasionally from house rules.
Give one command at a time and reward compliance.	Give a command if you cannot or will not enforce it.
Play the role of leader; you initiate activity.	Respond to your dog's demands.
Use the dog's name only when giving a command.	Use the dog's name without interacting.
Own all toys; take away all toys at the end of play time.	Let your dog think it owns the toys.
Take away anything your dogs steals, like food, socks, towels.	Fall for the "But it's so cute" routine.
Always call your dog to you to give affection.	Go to your dog to give affection.
Ignore demands to be picked up, petted, or cuddled.	Let your dog use submissive behaviour to dictate what it wants.
Feed your family before you feed your dog.	Give food from your table, ever, or let the dog clean the plates.
Decide your bed and furniture rules and stick to those rules.	Expect your dog to understand access to furniture *sometimes*.
Go through doors or passageways and down the stairs first.	Let your dog lead you.
Teach your dog to wait while you open doors, including car doors.	Let your dog barge through any door as soon as it is opened.
Teach the dog to gently take objects from your hands.	Allow the dog to snatch food or objects from you.
Teach your dog to eliminate on command.	Allow the dog to sniff endlessly and anoint every blade of grass.
Train your dog to walk nicely by your side.	Permit the dog to drag you where it wants to go.
Remember: a dog thinks like a dog.	Allow your emotional needs to put pressure on your dog.

2

Early Training

Dogs are always learning, but they learn best when they are young. This is a vital time for influencing your dog's future behaviour. Without your intervention, your dog will learn, but not what you want it to. Begin simple training the day your new canine companion arrives in your home. Provide it with a well-fitted collar, a private place to sleep, a designated play area, and suitable toys. These toys belong to you, the pack leader, and should not be left lying around. Your pup's mind is most open to new experiences when it is under 12 weeks old. The more it experiences now – children, cats, other dogs, joggers, cyclists, baby carts, cars, and public transport – the more it will take these things for granted. Ensure your pup learns as much as is necessary, while it is still young, to live the life you plan for it.

Early Home Routines

Start training your puppy as soon as you bring it into your home. Teach the puppy your rules before it makes its own. All family members should routinely handle a new puppy while it learns to wear a collar and lead, eat only from its own food bowl, sleep in its own bed, come when called, and wait on command. However, only one family member should be responsible for training.

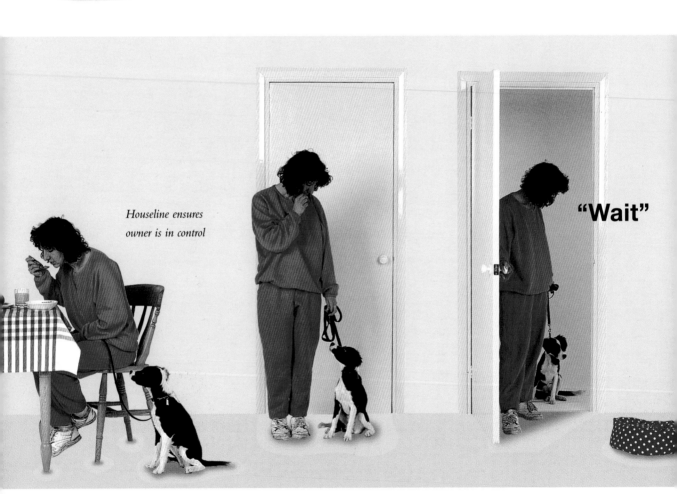

Houseline ensures owner is in control

"Wait"

Learning to wait

Your new puppy should learn that people eat before dogs, and are therefore more dominant members of the household, or pack.

Learning respect

A puppy must learn to obey the family in its new home, so all responsible family members should handle the puppy.

People go first

Dogs naturally want to rush through doors first. By teaching a puppy to wait and allow you to go first, you assert your authority over it. If the puppy does not understand this relationship, training can be difficult.

Additional information

The bed as a refuge

Dogs are curious and sociable animals, so do not isolate your new canine family members. Set up a dog bed as a personal space for the puppy, and place it in a busy area of the home, such as a corner of the kitchen.

Curious chewing

Puppies investigate their environment by tasting. They play by biting, but you should discipline the puppy when it nips by saying "No" firmly. Never reprimand the puppy by hitting it.

Bitter spray

A non-toxic, bitter-tasting spray is available from most veterinary surgeries and pet shops. Apply it to articles that you do not want the dog to chew, including your hands.

Positive enticement

By using food enticements rather than discipline, you will find it easier to teach the puppy more quickly which activities are not allowed.

A private place

Train the puppy to enjoy being left in a crate with its toys *(see page 44)*. Start by leaving it alone for short periods at first.

Basic Equipment

Choose accessories that are appropriate for the size and temperament of your dog, and replace collars frequently as your puppy grows. You will need a short lead, a long training lead, and an equally long, light houseline to use at home. Body harnesses, head halters, and muzzles are useful for certain types of dog *(see page 69)*.

Collars, leads, and muzzles

You should always have your dog under control, and this is particularly important during training. In addition to a standard lead, use a long cotton lead for outdoor training and a long houseline with a bolt snap for indoor control.

1 Leather lead
2 Reflective buckle collar
3 Large leather and nylon buckle collar
4 Quick-release flat collar
5 Rolled leather collar
6 Sight hound collar
7 Lead with tug ball
8 Extending lead
9 Check chain
10 Half-check collar
11 2-m (6-ft) cotton-webbing lead
12 Nylon cord houseline
13 Nylon cord longline
14 Fixed-noseband head halter
15 Adjustable-noseband head halter
16 Fabric muzzle
17 Basket muzzle
18 Fabric harness
19 Car harness

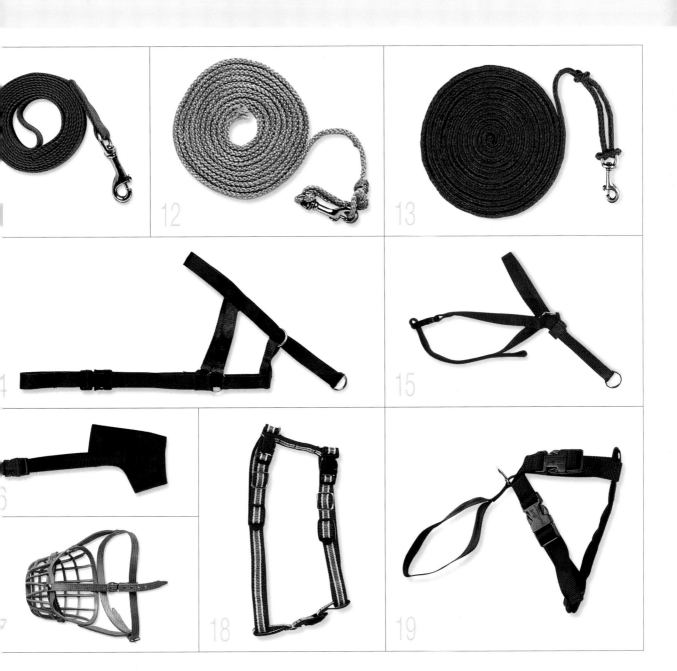

Additional equipment

Bean bags make excellent beds, while newspaper-lined playpens provide for playful activity and controlled house training. Crates should only be used for sleeping and quiet play. You should also keep some deterring equipment handy, such as a water pistol. You may need other equipment for your dog's particular training needs *(see page 120)*.

Grooming equipment

When it comes to grooming, you should always use equipment appropriate for the dog's coat type. Fast-growing coats, for example, require clipping or cutting, while heavy coats often need to be thinned out. It is best to train the dog from an early age to accept the sound of clippers and scissors. Nails, especially those of small, lightweight, and elderly dogs, need frequent attention. Unless there is a disease present, a puppy's teeth and ears are naturally clean. Later in life, however, these parts of the body benefit from routine cleaning. Train the dog while it is young to permit you to tend to these areas.

1 Water pistol	**10** Bean-bag bed	**19** Tooth-tartar remover
2 Training discs	**11** Thinning scissors	**20** Synthetic bristle brush
3 Clicker	**12** Slicker brush	**21** Nail cutters
4 Small squeaky toy	**13** Stripping comb	**22** Chamois cloth
5 Dog whistle	**14** Electric clippers	**23** Canine toothpaste
6 Shake bottle	**15** Wide-toothed comb	**24** Flea comb
7 Rubber brush	**16** Narrow-toothed comb	
8 Taste deterrent spray	**17** Soft pin brush	
9 Crate	**18** Toothbrush	

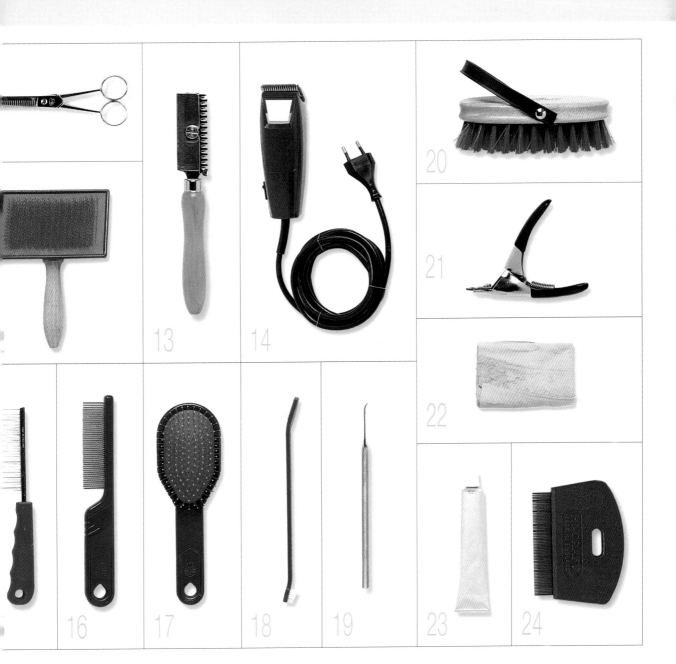

Daily Grooming

Grooming your dog daily not only keeps it clean and healthy, but also reasserts your authority over it. Picking up the dog, holding its head, and opening its mouth are dominant gestures, and they help to reinforce your control. Initially, use food rewards as distractions throughout the grooming sessions, then progress to verbal and physical praise alone.

Grooming preparations

Dog is on lead for assured control

Hand is placed, palm down, under dog's body

Picking up a dog
Pick up the dog by putting one arm around its chest and forelimbs, and the other around its rump. Place it on a table for grooming. You can ensure that the dog won't slip and injure itself by placing a rubber mat on the table.

Holding a dog still
Hold the dog in the stand position, and put your thumb through its collar. This will ensure that the dog doesn't move and that you are in control.

Special conditions

Long coats

Long-haired dogs with thick coats can develop mats under their legs. Take care when grooming these areas, since the skin here is often more sensitive than on other parts of the dog's body.

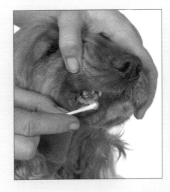

Lips and gums

Some breeds need to have their lip folds cleaned and their gums checked regularly. Use damp cotton-wool buds to remove any dirt.

Gentle brushing

Use long, firm strokes to brush along the dog's body. Brush the entire coat, including the tail and legs, avoiding any sensitive areas.

Turning a dog around

Place the flat of your hand, with the fingers together, over the hind-leg muscles, to turn the dog around. A flat palm avoids hurting the dog.

Special conditions

Hairy ears

Use a damp cotton-wool bud to clean the dog's ears, but be careful not to insert the bud into the ear canal. Carefully remove excess hair using forceps or your fingers.

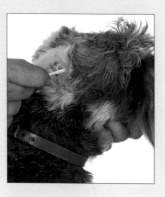

Foot maintenance

Minimize the risk of dirt embedding between the dog's toes by clipping and examining after exercise.

Grooming

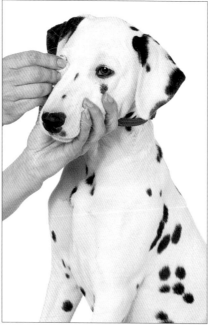

1 Trimming the nails

Cut the nails after the dog has been bathed, when its nails will be softer than usual. Take care not to cut the living tissue (the pink area inside the nail). If in doubt, ask a vet.

2 Cleaning the eyes

Many dogs build up mucus in the corners of their eyes. Holding the head firmly, bathe the eyes, using a clean piece of damp cotton wool for each one.

3 Examining the mouth

Use food rewards while training the dog to let you open and examine its mouth. You should check the dog's teeth and gums once a week.

Suitable Toys and Chews

Puppies chew objects in order to learn about their environment, but chewing can be an expensive problem for a dog's owner. By encouraging your dog to chew only its own specific toys, you will prevent it from damaging other household items. Always choose safe toys, and limit their availability to prevent the dog from becoming possessive of them.

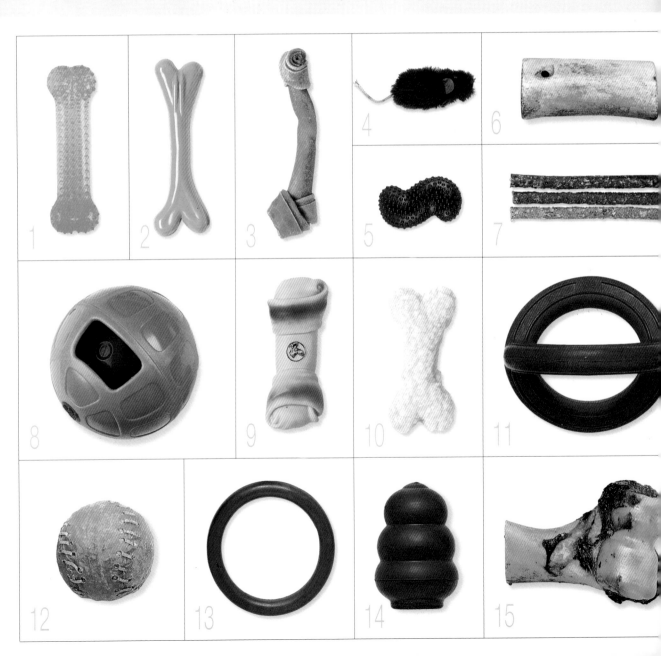

1 2 3 4 6 5 7 8 9 10 11 12 13 14 15

Types of toy

The best dog toys have their own unique smells and are unlike anything else a dog might find.

1 Bone to help clean teeth
2 Rubber bone
3 Rawhide chew
4 Squeaky mouse toy
5 Tartar-removing toy

6 Sterilized hollow bone
7 Coloured chew sticks
8 Activity toy
9 Plastic bone
10 Soft toy bone
11 Rubber tug toy
12 Rawhide ball
13 Rubber ring
14 Hollow chew toy for stuffing

15 Pressure-cooked bone
16 Rope ball
17 Tennis-ball tugger
18 Frisbee ®
19 Dental rope
20 Tug toy
21 Ball-on-a-rope
22 Rope tugger
23 Throw ball

New Experiences

Provide your puppy with as many experiences as possible. If you have your own garden, begin training in it as soon as you can. With your vet's approval, take your puppy to public places so that it becomes accustomed to traffic noise, people who look different to you, and car journeys. More importantly, your puppy will get used to obeying you in different environments and circumstances.

Puppy learns to socialize with other dogs

Playing with other dogs

Taking your puppy to weekly, supervised puppy classes *(see page 170)* will allow it to learn what canine body language means and how it can use body language when communicating with other dogs.

Outdoor rendezvous

Arrange for the dog to meet new people inside your home first, and then outdoors. This will prepare the dog for later meetings with people who will try to stroke it without asking your permission.

Ask your friends to sit on their haunches when greeting the puppy, so that they do not intimidate it. They can also offer a food treat, so that the puppy will learn to welcome approaches from other people.

Additional information

First outdoor experience

It is important for a puppy to safely experience the smells, sights, and sounds of everyday life from as early an age as possible. Carry your puppy outdoors before it is fully inoculated, but do not put it on the ground.

Frightening strangers

A person with a beard, a hat, or a different skin complexion to the dog's human family can be intimidating. Set up meetings between your friends and the dog, and reward the dog when it shows curiosity but remains calm.

Reward quiet behaviour

After a car journey, give food rewards and verbal praise if the dog displays no signs of agitation. Go for short drives initially, and gradually increase their duration. Always reward the dog for settling down and and remaining quiet.

A positive approach

Always instruct children to approach the dog quietly and to stroke it gently from the side. Make sure you reward the dog with verbal praise or a food treat when it behaves calmly.

Introducing the car

The back of a car can be a frightening place, especially if the dog's first experience in it causes motion sickness and nausea. Before actually driving anywhere, entice the dog into your parked car with a food reward. Once the dog is happy to sit in the car, accustom it to the sound of the engine. Train the dog to look upon the car as a second home *(see page 154)*.

Crate Training

It might look like a jail to you, but to the dog that has been trained from puppyhood to use it, a crate becomes a favourite place, the dog's own secure haven. Crates should be pleasant places and should never be used for discipline. Crate training encourages house training, reduces potentially destructive behaviour, and eases travelling with your dog.

1 Before starting crate training, place soft bedding, a bowl of water, and an interesting toy inside the crate. Using a tasty snack and the verbal command "Go to your crate", entice the puppy into its new home. Ensure that the door remains open so that the puppy can leave the crate at any time.

2 Once the puppy has become accustomed to the crate, it will continue to use it without any prompting from you. While the puppy plays contentedly, close the crate door for a few minutes. Keep the crate in a busy place like the kitchen.

Added benefits

Personal transport

Problems with travelling are eased if you have a crate-trained puppy. When confined to its own crate, this puppy feels secure in the car.

Not for punishment

Never send a dog to its crate in response to some misdemeanour as you might send a child to his room. A dog's attitude to its crate must always be positive.

Crate size

Crates should be big enough for the puppy to stand up and turn around, but not so big that it might use one end as a toilet. Most puppies do not soil their own bedding, so crating with plenty of toileting breaks also helps with house training.

Having become accustomed to its crate, this puppy is content to be confined to a playpen. Some dogs, especially rescued ones, will not tolerate crate confinement, but this rarely happens with puppies. Eventually the relaxed puppy will fall asleep in the security of its crate. However, even fully crate-trained puppies should not be left in crates for more than two hours during the day, and they should always be exercised before confinement. If the playpen is lined with newspaper, puppies can meet and play without causing havoc in your home.

House Training

If you have an adult dog that has never been house trained, treat it as you would a new puppy. Never punish your dog for making a mess in your home, since this only teaches it to be nervous and wary of you. Instead, anticipate when your dog needs to eliminate. After your dog wakes up, eats, or plays, take it to the place that you have chosen for it to relieve itself, and always clean up after it.

Toilet training

Training the puppy to use newspaper indoors can be confusing to it, since it learns that eliminating indoors is acceptable. Whenever possible, train the puppy to eliminate in an outdoor area, but if you have to use paper indoors, use crate timing *(opposite)* before you let the puppy out on to its newspaper.

Problem solving

Automatic reflex

Avoid accidents in the home by restricting the dog to its crate until you take it out to eliminate. As your dog relieves itself, use words like "Hurry up", then praise it. Soon your dog will eliminate when you give the "Hurry up" command.

Pointless punishment

Control your temper while you are house training a puppy. Scolding the dog is pointless unless you actually see it eliminating indoors. If you do, say "No" sternly, and move the puppy to its designated spot.

Prevent accidents from occurring by constantly supervising the puppy. If direct supervision is not possible, it is best to keep the puppy in its crate.

2 Dogs actively avoid soiling their personal quarters. Restrict the puppy to its crate whenever you are busy, and provide it with a toy to chew. Monitor the puppy's crate time, taking it out to relieve itself when necessary. Make sure that the crate is the correct size for the puppy; if it is too big, the puppy may soil it.

3 A puppy will need to eliminate after sleeping and playing, and especially after eating or being restricted to its crate. As a general rule, remember that a three-month-old puppy needs to eliminate every three hours.

Additional information

Responsible behaviour

Dog faeces are not only a public health hazard to people and to other dogs, they are also an aesthetic hazard to the environment. Ensure good relations with the community by always cleaning up after your dog. When you take the dog to a public place, remember to carry a poop scoop, or a simple plastic bag. Whenever possible, use biodegradable bags.

Anticipation

A dog that suddenly puts its nose down and sniffs intently is usually signalling that it is about to eliminate. Commercial spray products, which induce the puppy to use a designated area, are available from most pet stores.

Instant praise

When taking the puppy outside, keep its attention on you by talking to it or showing it toys to ensure that there are no accidents on the way. Say "Hurry up" as the puppy eliminates, then praise it for its good behaviour.

Acclimatization

Location, location, location

House training is easier and successful sooner when a dog is restricted to only one part of the house. Baby gates and crates are ideal for temporarily restricting a dog to a single location. As house training progresses, gates and crates can be moved to different rooms.

Doggy bed

Your dog's bed is its own secure space. Never send the dog to its bed as a form of punishment. Getting out of bed can be a signal that the dog needs to relieve itself. Make sure that, when the dog stays with friends or is kennelled, its bed goes with it. It ensures a feeling of security.

Coming to You

Begin this exercise when your puppy is alert and hungry. Divide your pet's meal into ten equal portions, and throughout the day entice it to the food bowl by using its name and the command "Come". Never recall the puppy to discipline it or do anything it might perceive as unpleasant, like giving it a pill, since it will associate returning to you with a disagreeable experience.

"Polly come"

Stand a short distance away from the puppy, in a quiet room with no distractions. A hallway is an ideal location. With a food treat visible in your hand, speak the puppy's name and, as it begins to move forwards, give the command "Come".

Problem solving

The tired dog

Dogs – and puppies in particular – have short attention spans and training is mentally exhausting for them. Train for only five to 15 minutes at a time, and never when the dog is tired. You should also plan training periods to occur before the dog embarks on active exercise, so that it is mentally and physically prepared for the session. Varying the places in which you train the dog helps maintain its interest.

The distracted dog

If the dog does not respond to a food reward, alter its feeding routine, giving fewer meals (but larger quantities). If it still does not respond well to food treats, try using a favourite squeaky toy as a reward.

The wilful dog

If the puppy is strong-willed, always carry out any training exercise with it on a lead. This ensures that you can always attract the puppy's attention and reminds it that it must listen and respond.

Bent knees bring treat closer to puppy

"Good dog to come"

As the puppy moves towards you, praise it by saying the words "Good dog" using a bright and enthusiastic tone of voice. Encourage the puppy to come directly to you by bending your knees and opening your arms wide.

As the puppy approaches, kneel down to get closer to its level. Praise the puppy again with words, stroking, and the food reward. In order to maintain the interest of the dog, vary the locations in which the training takes place.

Coming to You Outdoors

Once your dog has learned to come to you indoors, you can begin training with a collar and longline before moving to a more distracting location outdoors. Your dog's safety depends on you, so only when you are totally confident that the dog will come to you on command should you move on to recalling without the lead. Never recall your dog to discipline it.

"Sit"

Put a large knot at one end of a longline, with the clip attached to the dog's collar. Give the "Sit" command and stand on the dog's left-hand side, holding the shortened line in your right hand. Place your left foot firmly on the line, as close as possible to the knot.

Release the dog, letting out the longline gradually as the dog moves forwards. Be careful to do this in time with the speed of the dog's movement so the dog is not pulled up before it gets to the end of the line. Make sure the dog's legs do not become entangled in the line.

Additional information

Praise on return

Always greet your dog when it returns to you, no matter how long it takes it to get there. You are praising the very last thing the dog did, which was to come to you.

Lead in pocket

Do not brandish your lead when calling your dog – you are advertising that you will be putting the lead on and that the fun may be over. Get into the habit of simply touching the dog's collar on return. Do not grab the dog.

Make returning fun

Recall your dog several times during a walk, give a reward for compliance, and then release it to go and play again. Whenever the dog returns, play a game with a tug toy to make coming back worthwhile.

KEY TRAINING	
Coming to You	50
Sit	54

"Macy come"

"Good dog"

Line is kept firmly under your foot

Dog is welcomed with open arms

As the dog approaches the end of the line, call its name in a clear, friendly voice. You may need to move the weight of your body forwards to counteract any tension from the dog's pull. You are in control as long as your foot is firmly on the line.

When your dog hears its name, together with the "Come" command, it will turn around and begin to walk towards you. As it moves forwards, say "Good dog" in a welcoming voice. When the dog reaches you, kneel down with your arms open in the greeting position.

Sit and Lie Down

Once your puppy responds well to the command to come *(see page 50)*, you can begin teaching it to sit and to lie down. To ensure that you are always in control, you should practise the following exercise with the puppy on the lead. On completing this routine successfully, your puppy will be able to carry out a sequence of commands for the first time.

The "Sit" Command

"Polly come"

Owner holds food in front of body

"Sit"

"Good sit"

1 Facing the puppy, move away with the lead in your left hand and a food treat in your right. Keeping calm and trying not to excite the puppy, tell it to come to you as you show it the food.

2 When the puppy reaches you, slowly move the treat up and over its head. The puppy will sit in order to keep its eyes on the food. Give the command "Sit" as it starts to bend its hind legs.

3 Reinforce the "Sit" command from the front and to the side of the puppy. Reward each response with verbal praise and food treats. Gradually reduce the food rewards until words alone are sufficient.

Problem solving

Refusing to sit

If the puppy will not sit for a food treat, hold its collar with one hand and tuck its hindquarters under with the other, giving the "Sit" command as you do so. Reward the puppy with praise.

Refusing to lie down

Kneel down with the puppy sitting at your left. Place your palms under its forelegs (but do not grip them), and raise it up to a begging position and then into a lying position. Praise the puppy.

KEY TRAINING

Coming to You   50

The "Down" Command

*Lead is held firmly
under knees*

"Down"

*Food is held firmly
to prevent snatching*

"Good
down"

Once the puppy is sitting, kneel at its right side and hold its collar in your left hand. Holding a food treat in your right hand, place your hand on the puppy's nose before moving it downwards.

As the puppy's nose follows the treat, move it forwards to the front of its body. The moment the puppy starts to lie down, give the command "Down", but do not reward the puppy yet.

Move the food just far enough forwards to lure the puppy to lie down. Reward the puppy with praise and the food treat. Repeat the exercise frequently, until the puppy responds to words alone.

Walking without a Lead

Outdoor activities are a delight when your dog walks obediently by your side. It is often easiest to train a puppy to walk to heel off the lead at first, since it will enjoy human companionship and will usually be willing to follow its owner. Since most puppies also follow the scent of food snacks, it is useful to carry treats throughout training, so you can reward obedience.

"Heel"

"Heel"

"Steady"

Puppy foll treat inten

1 Walking in a straight line, with the puppy following the scent of the food reward in your right hand, give the command "Heel". Keep your left hand low, ready to grasp the puppy's collar.

2 Bending your knees and holding the food near to the puppy's nose, make a right turn, repeating the "Heel" command. The puppy must speed up in order to walk around you.

3 To turn left, use your left hand to guide the puppy by the collar, and issue the command "Steady". Hold the treat low down and move your right hand to the left. The puppy should follow.

Problem solving

Enjoyable training
If the puppy is not interested in a certain food reward, try using another, or switch to a favourite squeaky toy. Always keep training sessions short, no more than a few minutes at a time, and end them with a period of enjoyable play.

Using toys
If the puppy does not respond to food lures, try drawing its attention to a favourite toy.

Using a longline on the puppy should help ensure its compliance to your commands.

"Wait"

4 If, for any reason, the puppy's becomes distracted and its attention starts to wander, put your left hand under its collar, gently lure it back to the correct heel position, and continue with the exercise.

5 Give the command "Wait" and kneel to the puppy's right side. Hold the snack low to discourage jumping. Put your left hand, palm down, underneath the puppy's body to prevent it from moving.

Walking on a Lead

Your puppy's safety and wellbeing depend on you. A dog should never be allowed to run free unless it is under your supervision in a protected environment, away from danger. You should have already trained your puppy to sit and lie down while wearing a lead *(see page 54)* and to walk with you without wearing a lead *(see page 56)*. Now you can teach it to walk on the lead without pulling.

"Sit"

"Heel"

1 The training for this exercise should start indoors. Let the puppy look at and smell the lead. Then attach the lead to the puppy's well-fitting, comfortable collar *(see page 32)*.

2 With the puppy on your left side, hold the lead and a food reward in your right hand. Your left hand holds the slack, ready to slide down to the collar. Give the puppy the "Sit" command.

3 Begin to walk with your left foot first. As the puppy walks beside you, give the command "Heel". If the puppy surges forward, slide your left hand down the lead to its collar and gently pull backwards.

Problem solving

Climbing up the lead

If the puppy tries to jump up or climb the lead, sternly say "No" or "Off". Move away, give the "Sit" command, and start again. Do not train on outdoor walks at first – they can be too distracting. Train indoors, and slowly try busier locations.

Collapsing

If the puppy refuses to move, gently and patiently entice it with a favourite squeaky toy. Do not pull the puppy, or become angry with it. Instead, you should encourage the puppy with praise, and allow it to build up its confidence.

Pulling forwards

Every time the puppy pulls on the lead, stop. Lure it back beside you before stepping off. Neither you nor the puppy should lose concentration. If your dog is particularly boisterous, use a head halter *(see page 69)*.

"Good sit"

"Heel"

"Steady"

Owner holds puppy back by its collar

When the puppy is in the heel position, give the reward and verbal praise. Then command the puppy to sit. Slowly increase the distance you cover as the puppy obeys the sequence of commands.

Once the puppy is able to walk to heel and sit obediently as you go from room to room, you can train it to turn right. Guide it around to the right with your left hand, and give the command "Heel".

To make a left turn, increase your own speed and hold the food in front of the puppy's nose to slow it down. Keep the puppy close to your left leg and give the "Steady" command as it slows down.

Hands-Free Training

Untrained dogs, by nature, pull on their leads. To control them, owners tend to pull back. The resulting tension on the lead is pointless and counterproductive, since dogs quickly accept it as the normal state of affairs. By training your dog to walk on a lead with this "hands-free" method, you eliminate the risk of unwittingly training the dog to pull when it is on the lead.

Train in a quiet place. Attach a 6-ft lead to your dog's collar, but, instead of holding the lead, leave it lying on the floor. Get your dog's attention with a favourite food or toy treat.

With your left foot, start to walk forwards. The dog will move too, drawn by your movement. When its shoulders start to move past your left leg, stop suddenly and silently, stepping on the lead.

Your dog is brought to an abrupt halt. He may at first appear bewildered by what has happened and will turn to look at you. Smile and lure him back with the treat in your hand.

Problem solving

Indoor first

This method of lead control takes a little practice. Start in a hallway until you feel comfortable using your foot to control the lead. Make sure you gently place your foot on the lead instead of stamping on it.

No hands

Remember to keep your hands off the lead and a smile on your face. Your foot on the lead means you are in control. If you have a strong dog, a few knots along the line of the lead will prevent the lead from slipping under your foot.

Make it positive

Remember that – as far as the dog is concerned – the tightened lead has nothing to do with you. Wait for the dog to come back by your side. Walk forwards only when you have its attention and there is no tension on the lead.

Encourage your dog to return to your side by using welcoming gestures and friendly body language as well as the treat. Be as flamboyant as you need without overexciting your dog.

When the dog returns, reward it. Repeat the exercise, this time stopping and luring the dog back before it gets to the end of the lead. When the dog responds well indoors, move training outdoors.

Lead Training Problems

Puppies that have been allowed to run to the end of their leads and investigate the world without control from their owners can turn into easily distracted dogs. These dogs often chew their leads, tow their owners, investigate every object on the ground, tear after other dogs, and refuse to comply with their owners' commands. Easily distracted dogs need to learn lead manners.

The problem

The remedy

Climbing and chewing

To young and boisterous dogs, leads are exciting new toys. These dogs sometimes chew their leads in a playful way, or even try to climb them.

Spray the lead

Make the lead unpleasant to chew by spraying it with a bitter-tasting liquid *(see page 31)*. When the dog tries to chew or climb the lead, it is disciplined by the unpleasant taste, rather than by you.

Problem solving

No race

Keep your dog interested in being with you. Let it know that you have its favourite toy or treat, and reward good walking behaviour. If your dog tows you, walk in the opposite direction. Do not let it race you anywhere.

No drag

Try to find out why your dog lies down and refuses to walk. Make sure there is nothing in the dog's immediate environment at the basis of its fear – a backfiring car, for example, can make a dog think that its immediate environment is attacking it. Walking with another steady dog can often help overcome this situation. If your dog refuses to walk, loosen the pressure on its collar and encourage it forwards.

The problem

The remedy

Collapsing submissively

While some dogs collapse because they are intimidated when brought back to the heel position, others regard it as a game, and roll over in play.

Use a toy

If the dog collapses on the ground, take a step or two backwards, and then use a favourite toy to excite the dog and induce it to get up.

You are on a Lead too

Many dog owners find themselves playing tug-of-war with their dogs. When the dogs pull forwards, they instinctively pull back. This is the wrong approach. Remember you are in control. Use common sense rather than physical force. Anticipate your dog's behaviour and, when it thinks about pulling, interrupt its thoughts by luring its body and mind back where you want them.

Be aware of your own body movement

Keep your hands near your body, not waving in the air. Do not let the lead go slack, but do not keep active tension on it either. You want your dog to subtly feel your presence. When your dog seems intent on chasing a cat or another dog, react and respond while it is still thinking about what it is going to do. Do not get tense. Stand straight and remain physically relaxed with your hands down but with one foot in front of the other. This gives stability, which comes from the centre of your body. Do not pull on your dog's collar, since this can trigger an aggressive reaction.

Problem solving

Guide

Think of your lead as a guide, not a restraint. Use it to train your dog and, when necessary, to ensure its safety. In appropriate circumstances, however, remember to give your dog the off-lead freedom to be a dog.

Lead-dependent

Some dog owners think that – as long as they feel tension on the lead – they are in control of the dog. However, these people fail to understand that real control comes from their relationship with their dog, the dog's understanding of their commands, and its willingness to respond, rather than having to comply because it is on a lead.

Lure your dog away

Do not let your dog stare at whatever is distracting it and do not let it pull the lead taut. Get into the habit of carrying a toy when you are out with your dog. Use the toy to create a diversion, turning the dog's head away from the sight or activity that causes it to pull on its lead.

Work with your dog, not against it

When your dog meets another, remain relaxed but aware, ready to turn away if necessary. Make sure that your dog does not feel a taut, tight lead, because this could produce body language from it that might trigger a confrontation with the other dog.

3

Further Training

A reliable response to simple commands – come, sit, stay, down – is at the very heart of dog training. You and your dog should routinely practise basic obedience training. It remains the basis of all further training. This is vital because there are always potentially dangerous circumstances where your dog's interest will be distracted. Reliable control over your dog can literally be life-saving. The range of personalities in dogs is wonderful. This is one of their attributes we find so appealing, but it also means that not all dogs respond to the same training methods. Choose the method of control and restraint most suitable for both of you. Modify your training method as necessary, but always keep training short, kind, and fun.

Control and Restraint

It is essential that you use an appropriate form of control when training your dog, and especially when you are in any public place. Most dogs respond to the pull of a half-check collar, but others are more responsive to head halters or harnesses. Also, where laws or common sense dictate, make sure that your dog wears a muzzle *(see pages 32)*.

Half-check collar

1 Make sure you position your dog's half-check collar correctly around its neck – the soft webbing should be around the dog's throat and the chain links should be over the top of its neck.

2 Pull upwards on the lead to tighten the collar. This controls unwanted activity in most dogs without causing discomfort. Avoid using check collars on dogs with delicate windpipes.

Muzzling a dog

Fastening a muzzle

Kneel beside the dog and position the muzzle from below its head. Pull the straps gently behind the dog's neck and fasten them. The muzzle should fit securely while allowing the dog to open its jaws and pant freely.

First-time use

The dog may try to take off the muzzle at first. You should never attempt to remove the muzzle while the dog is pawing at it. Instead, distract the dog and remove the muzzle when it has quietened down. Muzzled dogs should not be left unsupervised for long periods of time. Muzzling not only prevents the dog from scavenging and minimizes the risk of bites, but also reminds it that you are in control.

Head halter

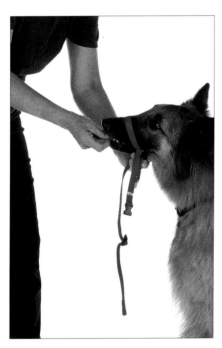

1 Slip the head halter over the dog's muzzle, putting your hand under its jaw to hold its head up. Luring the dog into the halter with a titbit makes the experience more pleasant.

2 Fasten the halter behind the dog's neck, making sure that it is not too tight. You should be able to get two fingers under any part of the halter.

3 Attach the lead to the halter ring under the dog's lower jaw. If the dog pulls forward, its own momentum pulls its head down.

Problem solving

Appropriate equipment
Whatever equipment you choose for your dog should be appropriate to that breed, and you should feel comfortable using it. Never use equipment that causes the dog pain. Equipment incorrectly used can also cause harm.

Accepting head halters
Choose a head halter that fits about halfway down the dog's face – preferably with an adjustable noseband. This should fit snugly, not tightly, and should not ride up around the dog's eyes. Dogs take time to get used to head halters.

Letting the dog eat with the halter on helps it accept the halter. Do not put sustained pressure on the head halter. Train the dog to walk both sides with the halter so its neck muscles are not stretched on one side only. Never take off a halter while

a dog is trying to get it off itself. Make it more difficult for the dog to remove it with its paws, by looping the clip of the halter back through the dog's flat collar. Remove the halter when the dog is settled.

Body harnesses

Emergency harness
Loop the lead across the dog's chest and hold it close to its body. This enables you to retain firm control of the dog if it becomes frightened and pulls unexpectedly.

Standard harness
With the harness correctly positioned, the dog is controlled by tension to the ribcage. A harness is suitable for breeds with soft windpipes, such as Yorkshire terriers, and for those with muscular necks, such as pugs.

Sit and Stay

The commands "Sit" and "Stay" form the basis of responsible pet ownership and are useful forms of control during outdoor activity. Begin training in a quiet indoor area, such as a hallway, and limit each session to 15 minutes. Once your dog has learned to respond consistently to your word commands, you will be able to advance to using simple hand signals (*see page 78*).

"Sit"

Lead is held at waist level

"Stay"

Food treat is palmed but obvious

1 Hold the telescoped lead in your left hand and a treat in your right. As the dog sits, concentrating on the treat, command it to "Sit".

2 Maintaining tension on the lead, step forwards with your right foot. Give the "Stay" command as you move forwards.

3 Move your left foot to join your right foot, remembering to keep gentle eye contact with the dog at all times.

4 Exerting light pressure on the lead, held over the dog's head, turn to face the dog. Keep its attention by holding the food up high.

Problem solving

Greedy dog

Some dogs are very food-oriented. If this is the case with yours, you may find that using food in the stays is too tempting. You will need to judge when and when not to let the dog know that you have a treat.

If the dog moves

You are teaching your dog a completely new language. Do not expect it to understand the commands immediately. If the dog moves, hold it by the collar with your left hand and tuck its bottom down with your right.

"Good stay"

Food reward is held up to maintain eye contact

5 Reward the dog for staying. Now slowly walk around the dog, holding the lead above its head. Issue as few commands as possible, so that you do not confuse the dog.

6 After several sessions, the dog should sit and stay while on the lead. Now drop the lead and repeat each of the previous five steps, always praising the dog for good behaviour.

7 When the dog sits and stays with the lead dropped, give it the treat. Reward the dog while it is doing what it is told, not afterwards. End the training by opening your arms and saying "OK".

Come and Sit

You will often notice potential dangers before your dog does, so teaching it to return to you on command is essential for its safety. As a puppy your dog comes to you for security, but as an adult it should be trained to return because it wants to be with you. Recall training is rewarding and fun, and the best results are obtained when a reliable bond has been established between you and your dog.

"Stay"

"Prince come"

"Sit"

1 The dog should have previously learned to sit and stay. With the lead in your left hand and a food treat in your right, walk away from the dog, always giving the command "Stay".

2 Once you are as far away as the lead will allow, still holding the lead, turn to face the dog. Show it the food treat. Call the dog, using its name in addition to the command "Come".

3 As the dog reaches you, give the "Sit" command. Many dogs will naturally sit in order to keep an eye on the reward, but you should still issue the command as the dog sits.

Additional information

Have patience

The "Sit", "Stay", and "Come" commands are the most important lessons you can teach a dog, since they enable you to keep it under control at all times. All dog owners have a responsibility to ensure that their pets are not a nuisance. Make sure you always praise the dog when it responds well – and use a positive tone of voice when you do so. When it does not obey a command, repeat the exercise from the previous level of success.

Have fun

Training should be fun for both of you. Use rewards freely at first and soon the dog will come to you because it enjoys your company. Finish training sessions with games or play, so that the dog will look forward to the next lesson.

"Prince come"

"Good dog to come"

Longline is slack but ensures compliance with command

4 Once the dog has learned to return to you on a standard lead, move on to a longline. Instead of a food treat, use a toy reward, since that will be the most visible to the dog from a distance.

5 When the dog obediently responds to the "Come" and "Sit" commands, give it the toy reward and praise it. Eventually your dog will be able to carry out this exercise without a lead.

Lie Down

Training your dog to lie down on command is a valuable lesson, especially during outdoor activities where there are dangers such as busy roads. Your dog will also learn that you are in control, which is particularly important if it is a dominant individual. There are two lying positions: sphinx, in which the hind legs are tucked under, and flat, where the hips are rolled and the legs are to one side.

"Down"

1 With the dog on the lead on your left side, command it to sit. Kneel down and tuck the lead under your knees. Hold the dog's collar with your left hand and a food reward in your right palm.

2 With the food hidden in your closed fist, let the dog smell the scent. This focuses the dog's mind, while your hand under the collar prevents the dog from moving forwards.

3 Make an L shape in the air with your right hand by moving it straight down, then forwards between the dog's forepaws. As the dog drops to follow the food, issue the command "Down".

Problem solving

Reluctant dogs

If the dog is not food-oriented, try changing the reward to a chew toy. Only physically assist dogs into the down position *(see page 55)* if they accept being touched. Use only rewards if you have a dominant dog.

Reinforcing the down

If the dog's shoulders rise from the down position before it has been released, run your hand firmly along the lead to the collar. This controls the upwards movement, and exerts downwards pressure. As the dog goes back down, repeat "Down". The dog should only leave this position when you say "OK".

"Down"

4 As soon as the dog lies down, reward it with the food treat. If your dog is not food oriented, try this exercise with a favourite chew toy. At this stage, it does not matter which position the dog assumes, as long as it is comfortable.

Emergency action: instant down position

Kneel, slide your hand down the lead to the collar, and pull down, giving the command "Down". Praise the dog when it is in the down position. Train the dog indoors or in a quiet area with few distractions. Once it has mastered the lesson, move to a more stimulating environment.

Down and Stay

Jumping up on people and chasing are all part of natural dog behaviour, but they can be unpleasant and even dangerous activities. By teaching your dog to stay on command you can control these unwanted actions. Continue to use verbal commands and rewards, but this is also a good time to introduce simple hand signals so that your dog can understand your commands from a distance.

"Stay"

1 With the dog in the down position on your left side, issue the command "Stay". Holding the lead in your right hand, move your left hand, palm flat, down towards the dog, and walk away.

2 Maintain eye contact with the dog, and hold the lead loosely as you walk away. Do not use a food reward when training the dog to stay down, since it will want to come to you for it.

3 Still maintaining eye contact, turn, stand still, and say "Good stay". Praise the dog. Gradually extend the duration of the down position until the dog stays down for several minutes.

Extra information

Practical uses

You should train the dog to remain lying down even when unexpected activity occurs around it. This ensures safety for the dog and for other people, while displaying its obedient behaviour.

Staying in your absence

Gradually increase the distance between you and your dog while you are still in its sight, moving around while the dog stays down. Only when the dog is totally relaxed should you attempt to briefly go out of sight.

"Good stay"

"Good stay"

"OK"

4 After a few minutes, return to the dog and give the verbal reward "Good stay". Do this calmly and quietly while the dog is still lying down. Do not excite it, and do not reward it for getting up.

5 Show the dog your open palm and release it with the word "OK". Do not offer any more praise after you have released the dog, since the praise must be for the exercise, not the release.

Settling Down

Training your dog to chill out is not as silly as it seems. A dog that willingly lets you lift its front legs off the ground, rolls over exposing its belly, or "begs" is relaxed and compliant with people. Also, a dog that is trained to relax is easier to groom and, from my perspective as a practising vet, much easier to examine. Both puppies and adult dogs can be trained to "settle down".

Calming high spirits

Gradual exercises develops your confidence in handling the dog and its confidence in being handled by you. With your dog on your lap, lift its forepaws and draw it back until it is resting on its back on your lap.

Front legs off the ground

Slowly draw the dog up from a sitting to a begging position. At first raise its front feet a few centimetres off the ground. Praise it when it relaxes. If it is tense, lower its feet back, but keep holding it until it relaxes.

Chill out

"Belly up" is a vulnerable position, and a dog's willingness to relax on its back, cradled by you, means it accepts your handling. Speak calmly and give a quiet release command at the end of the session.

Problem solving

No rush

Start to teach the relaxing position in an area with no distractions and when you have the time to be as calm as you want your dog to be. Never flip a dog over on its back. Work up to this position so the dog accepts it naturally.

Breed specific

Some dogs, like many sight hounds, find lying on their backs difficult and probably uncomfortable due to their build. Roll these dogs, and any dog with a back problem, over on their sides instead.

Gentle tickling

If you move your fingers at all, do so very slowly and very gently. Do not treat a dog's tummy as a washboard! Your aim is to make the exercise so pleasant that the dog goes to sleep.

Quiet release

When you break off this exercise, do it quietly and slowly rather than by jumping up. Give the dog a treat while it is lying down, quiet praise in the relaxing position, then give the release command and no more praise.

Subtle control

High-energy dogs benefit from active "settle-down" training. Sitting with your dog's lead under your foot prevents it from getting up to demand attention and forces it to relax. Settling down is an important training lesson that allows you to do what you want without unwanted canine demands.

The big chill

All dogs, large or small, enjoy relaxing with the pack leader, whether by natural inclination or through training. Fortunately, most pack leaders find chilling out with their dogs equally soothing.

Bark Control

A barking dog offers protection and makes a good burglar alarm, but you do need an on/off switch. By teaching your dog to "speak" on command, you will be able to control its barking and to command it to be quiet. Once the dog knows that barking is only allowed under specific circumstances, it can be trained to bark on hearing sounds like smoke alarms or noises outside a window.

"Good dog"

"Speak"

1 Attach the dog's lead to a fence or post, and stand about 1 metre (3 ft) away. Tease the dog by showing it a toy, and give it a food reward when it barks with frustration.

2 Put the toy away, and change the reward from a food treat to a verbal "Good dog" when the dog barks. Occasionally do give your dog a more gratifying food treat.

3 Give the command "Speak" the moment the dog barks, then give the toy as a reward. Good timing is essential – by observing the dog's body language you can anticipate the bark *(see page 20)*.

Additional information

Alternative "Quiet"

If the dog is food-oriented, put a tasty morsel of food on its nose to stop it from barking. Timing your command perfectly, say "Quiet" as the dog stops barking, then give the food treat. Only reward the dog when it is silent.

Protection

Most people only require their dog to bark as a means of defence, so they teach the command "Guard" rather than "Speak". A barking dog is a good deterrent against intruders in the home or potential attackers outdoors.

Attention seeking

All barking is essentially attention seeking. The dog that barks at everything that passes your window can be annoying. The dog may think he is standing guard, but he may also be bored. Keep the dog exercised and mentally stimulated and the boredom barking should stop.

"Quiet"

4 Once the dog understands "Speak", command it to be "Quiet" when it is barking. Give the toy reward as soon as it stops barking, but put the toy away and command "No" if it continues.

5 After teaching the dog to bark or be quiet when you are near, move a short distance away from it. Repeat the exercise from the beginning, until the dog learns to respond to the commands.

6 Return to the dog and reward it with its favourite toy. Train the dog until it consistently responds to intermittent rewards while tied to the fence. Then release it and train with it off the lead.

Separation Anxiety

Dogs that lack confidence, particularly individuals that have been through animal shelters, are the ones most likely to exhibit signs of separation anxiety – that is, to bark, dig, and destroy furniture and possessions when they are left alone. These insecure animals need gentle handling, and their anxiety-related activities will take time and patience to cure.

Attention-seeking howling

A dog left in a closed room may howl in protest or may try to destroy the door in a bid to get out. Never return to a barking dog. Wait until it is quiet before you release it and do not fuss when you do so. A baby gate *(see page 49)* allows the dog to see you without following you around.

A den is not a prison

Many dogs treat their indoor kennels as their dens and are very happy to be left in them for reasonable periods of time. Using an indoor kennel eliminates random chewing and destruction problems for the dog left alone. The dog should always have something to chew in its kennel.

Problem solving

No trigger

We can trigger separation anxiety without knowing it. Jangling your keys, telling the dog to be good, and saying "Goodbye" all tell the dog you are going. When you leave the house, do so quietly and quickly without discussion.

Mock departures

The dog should think your coming and going is just part of everyday life and not a threat. Jangle your keys as you move around the house. Go out and quickly return. Leave by various routes.

Lacking confidence

If your dog suffers from separation anxiety, gradually, over a period of many weeks, increase the periods of separation, always leaving the dog with a toy that you have rubbed with your hands. Discipline the dog only if you see it misbehaving – never after. Poor timing on your part will confuse the dog further.

Exercise first

A dog that is well exercised, fed, and watered will normally settle down to sleep when left on its own. Giving the dog an old article of the owner's clothing to curl up with can act as a pacifier, but be sure you do not leave clothes you value around for the dog to appropriate as well.

Own bed

Leave your dog comfortable in its own bed with something to chew. Limiting the dog's access to only certain areas of the house will keep it from sleeping where it is not allowed to or from appropriating its owner's property as solace until it has earned the privilege of unlimited house access.

Learning to Touch

Training a dog to use its paw teaches it dexterity, and some dogs are more adept at this than others. It is a way in which dogs can communicate, and it is also the basis for "shaking hands" – a valuable game, since raising a paw is a subservient gesture for a dog. By training your dog to carry out this exercise, you will be reinforcing your pack-leader status.

"Sit"

Dog is prevented from putting muzzle near food reward

1 With the dog on your left side, issue the command "Sit". Kneeling down, hold the dog's collar in your left hand, and show it the food you have concealed in your right hand.

2 Move your right hand down to the floor, until it is in front of the dog's paws. With your left hand, hold the collar to prevent the dog from following the scent of the treat and lying down.

3 Push the treat towards the dog's paws. As the dog lifts its paw, move your clenched hand under it, and then slightly up off the floor. Continue to restrain the dog by the collar.

Extra information

Touch Game

Once your dog has learned to use its paw, you can train it to open doors and play games. You can also teach the dog to work a lever which will trigger a toy or ball for it to catch. This is the basis of the dog sport "Flyball".

Excessive pawing

If the dog demands attention by pawing at you excessively, say "No" firmly and command it to lie down. Be aware, however, that by this behaviour the dog is letting you know that it needs mental and physical stimulation.

High ten

Once your dog has learned to touch your hand on command, begin to raise your hand above its head and encourage him to use one front paw in a "High five" or both paws in a "High ten" salute.

"Paw"

4 When the dog's paw rests on your fist, lift it up and issue the command "Paw". Then give the food reward. Repeat the exercise, using "Paw" to reward the response, instead of food.

5 Once the dog has learned to consistently raise its paw to your hand on verbal command alone, show it that you are concealing a food reward behind a small piece of plywood.

6 Issue the command "Paw", and reward the dog with the food treat when it touches the plywood. This is the basis for a variety of touch games which will keep your dog physically and mentally stimulated.

Walking to Heel

Before you train your dog to walk to heel, it should be able to sit obediently. Start training in the garden, and make sure there are no distractions. Increase the distractions until the dog pays attention to you while walking to heel around the whole garden. If your dog is powerful or boisterous, using a head halter will give you best control. Avoid constantly repeating the "Heel" command.

"Sit"

"Shep heel"

Lead is held in both hands

Light jerks on lead bring dog back into position

1. Put the dog in the "Sit" position on your left side. Hold the telescoped lead in both hands, and keep a food reward in your right hand. Hold the lead close to the dog's collar in your left hand.

2. Using the dog's name and the command "Heel", begin to walk forwards, leading with your left foot. Give the food reward to the dog when it has walked to heel successfully for a few paces.

3. When the dog is able to walk about 20 paces without restraint and without pulling on the lead, train it to turn right as you keep on walking by using a food reward as an incentive.

Heeling off the lead

Without a lead

When the dog has been successfully trained to walk to heel on the lead, repeat the exercise without the lead. Put the lead over your shoulder and hold a food reward in your right hand. Walk forward, giving the "Heel" command.

Right turn

To train the dog to make a right turn without the lead, keep it close to your left leg and hold the food reward in your right hand. Issue the "Heel" command and draw the dog to the right as it follows the food reward.

Left turn

Reaching across the front of your body with the food in your right hand, set off with your left foot to make a left turn. Give the command "Heel" as you do so. The dog will slow down in order to stay near the food.

"Shep heel"

Dog remains close to owner's thigh

4 To train your dog to make a left turn, slide your hand down the lead to the dog's collar and, leading with your left leg, increase your speed while slowing the dog for the turn.

5 Now make an about turn. Still using food to lure the dog, say the dog's name and give the command "Heel" while turning a full circle. The dog will follow the food reward.

Holding Objects

An enjoyable game you can play with your dog involves fetching objects *(see page 93)*. However, first the dog must learn to hold an object in its mouth. Do not use squeaky toys, since your dog will want to chew them. Use a small piece of rolled-up carpet or a retrieve dummy. Only reward with verbal and physical praise – not with food treats – since the dog must continue to hold the object.

Holding an object

"Good dog"

"Good hold"

"Good dog to hold"

1 Kneel beside the dog, who should be sitting. Hold the lead under your knees and your left arm around the dog's head. Gently open the dog's mouth with your thumb, saying "Good dog".

2 Having previously teased the dog with the training object, and after having made sure that it is not unhappy, hold the dog's head up and put the object into its mouth. Give the command "Good hold".

3 The dog should hold the training object willingly and correctly just behind its canine teeth, with its tongue retracted. Praise the dog by saying "Good dog to hold".

Problem solving

Difficult holds

Some dogs – Boxers, for example – have overshot jaws. In such cases, the dogs must hold objects in front of their canine teeth, rather than behind them.

Avoiding the object

If the dog turns its head away from the training object, follow the dog's head and make sure you always keep the object at nose level.

Picking up an object

"Good dog"

"Hold"

"Good hold"

4 Now teach the dog to pick up the object. Bring the object up to the dog's nose, then move it down towards the floor. The dog should follow the object intently. Give the verbal reward "Good dog".

5 Rest the object on the floor but do not take your hand away. Give the command "Hold" as the dog moves forward to take the object in its mouth.

6 Remove your hand from the object, and the dog should pick it up. At the same moment, repeat the command "Good hold", ensuring that the dog does not drop the object.

Retrieving Objects

Once your dog has learned to hold and pick up an object, it is ready to learn to chase it and bring it back to you. If you are training a puppy, use a squeaky toy initially and let the puppy play with it for a while first. Otherwise, use the same object that you used when training your dog to hold objects. These exercises offer your dog both mental and physical stimulation.

Stage one: Fetch

"Fetch"

Dog on lead is under owner's control

1 Use a brightly coloured object, such as a rolled-up piece of carpet or retrieve dummy, to attract your dog's attention. With the dog's lead attached for reliable control, hold the dog by its collar with one hand as you throw the object a short distance.

2 Give the command "Fetch" as you release your hold on the dog's collar. The dog will run towards the object and, having been trained to pick up and hold the familiar object *(see page 90)*, your dog should now chase it enthusiastically.

Problem solving

Chewing objects

If your dog chews its retrieve objects, retrain the "Hold" command *(see page 90)* until the dog learns to hold the object in a quiet mouth. Retrain the last thing first, beginning with the dog sitting in front of you quietly holding the object in its mouth. Give it gentle praise for holding, but no praise for chewing. Do not throw the object again until you have achieved a quiet hold.

Reluctant to fetch

Make the retrieve game more interesting for your dog by using a toy and running with the dog on its lead to where you have thrown the object. Gradually increase the distance you throw the toy.

Reluctant to hold

If the dog runs to the object but appears puzzled upon reaching it, the dog has not yet learned to hold properly. Teach the "Hold" command again *(see page 90)* using a toy that is more interesting to the dog.

Stage two: Come and Give

"Come"

"Good dog"

Dog remains standing

1 Once your dog has picked up the object, firmly give the command "Come" to recall it. As the dog turns round to move towards you, crouch down to encourage it and hold your hand out ready to take the object. If necessary, give gentle jerks on the lead.

2 Still crouching down, reward the dog for its obedience in coming to you with firm strokes down its side and also give it verbal praise using the words "Good dog". Put your hand under the dog's jaw to prevent it from dropping the object.

Reluctant to return

If your dog does not respond and obey when you give the command "Come", go back to recall training *(see page 50)* and practise this again before continuing with the retrieving objects exercise.

Puppy retrieving

You can turn this exercise into a game to play with a puppy. Let the puppy chew the toy, and do not try to take it away. However, when the puppy drops the object of its own accord, you should praise it enthusiastically.

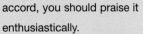

"Thank you"

"Sit"

3 While still holding the object, stand up and say "Thank you". As you do so, gently but firmly take the object from the dog's mouth. There is no more praise at this point, since praise after delivering the object often teaches a dog to spit out the object of its own volition. Your smile is its reward.

4 Reminding your dog that you are still in control, command it to "Sit". To encourage the dog to release the object when you say "Thank you" next time, give the object back to the dog as a final reward for completing this exercise successfully.

4

Playing Games

Virtually all of us consider our dogs to be members of the family, not human but not quite as "animal"

as other animals. Playing with our dogs is at the heart of this relationship, but we need to remember

that they play by different rules. Train your dog to play to our rules by understanding their natural

needs. Dogs thrive on mental as well as physical stimulation. Their pack mentality affects all aspects

of their behaviour – with us, with children, and with other dogs. It is easy and enjoyable to train

your dog to accept commands from your children by creating games for them to play that reinforce

the higher rank of your children. Choose games that are appropriate for the dog's size, weight, age,

and mental status. Tug-of-war, for example, should be avoided if you have a naturally dominant dog.

Dogs and Children

It is just as important to train children how to approach dogs as it is to train dogs how to behave with children. Teach your children that they should always ask the owner's permission before touching a dog. Instruct them never to rush up to a dog or to tease it or shout at it. Children should not be given responsibility for training or feeding a dog until they are mature and sensible.

Boy looks at owner and asks to stroke dog

No eye contact
You should make sure that children make eye contact with you rather than with the dog. Because children are smaller and less authoritative than adults, they are more at risk from bites.

Gentle strokes
Instruct children to stroke the dog from the side, not from the front, and tell them that they should never pat the dog's head. Praise the dog for its good behaviour, but be prepared to reprimand it if it snaps or growls through fear.

Problem solving

Meeting the baby

Allow the dog to see and smell, but not touch, a new baby. Praise, play with, and feed the dog in the baby's presence, but be aware that an infant's squeals and jerky movements can stimulate nervous behaviour.

Safety first

A dog should wear a muzzle in the presence of toddlers. This is particularly important if the dog guards or chases, if it has ever threatened or bitten anyone, or if it has not been well trained in obedience.

Exciting activity

Train the dog to lie down, even in the presence of exciting activity, such as children playing with a ball. Dogs naturally nip and chew in a playful context, so do not leave them alone with small children.

Dog is not frightened by children

Introduction to children

Allow a new dog to scent and investigate a child only if you are sure that the dog is a reliable individual, and, even then, such scenting and investigating should only be allowed in your presence.

Adult responsibilities

Only adult members of the household should feed the dog. Do not let children carry food near the dog. You should also bear in mind that young children should not walk the dog unless accompanied by an adult.

Games with Children

Sensible and responsible children thoroughly enjoy playing with well-trained, obedient dogs that willingly respond to their commands. The longline ensures that the dog is ultimately always under control. Do not let children play football games with your dog in public parks – the dog will want to join any group playing, and some footballers don't want canine team-mates.

Good control

As the girl throws the fetch toy, the dog becomes alert. A well-trained dog retrieves only when told to do so. Teaching games such as fetch are best done by adults. Children should participate only once the dog knows exactly what to do.

Adult supervision

The child takes the retrieved toy watched by an adult. Until a child is emotionally mature and is fully able to understand how to behave with and control a dog, all play activities with any dog, should always be supervised by an adult.

Additional information

No mouth games

Children should never play mouth games with dogs. Dogs have 42 teeth and children have ten fingers – a very bad ratio. Encouraging dogs to play mouth games can put the dog higher than the child in pack order – this should be avoided.

No games of strength

Playing tug games with a dog has a real potential for disaster for children. Most children will make very strong eye contact in a pulling contest and this can be seen by the dog as being seriously confrontational.

No shared toys

Children's toys are children's toys, and dogs should not share them. If necessary, use a bitter-tasting deterrent spray *(see page 31)* to discourage dogs from appropriating children's toys.

No teasing

Teasing a dog with food is unfair and will inadvertently teach a dog to snatch food from a child's hand.

Tiny leaders

As the child takes the toy, she gives the dog a food reward. By playing games with all your family, your dog learns that within the human pack in which it lives, children also have power and authority. It also learns that children are fun to play with.

Who owns that toy?

The dog must learn that all toys belong to humans, even small humans. At the end of any game your child should place the toy back in the toy basket in full view of the dog. In your dog's mind, this enhances your child's authority.

Games with Your Dog

Dogs thrive on both mental and physical stimulation. They are also inquisitive and enjoy human companionship. By playing constructive games with your dog, you can alleviate boredom, channel the dog's natural jumping behaviour, and reduce any destructive activity. By controlling the games, you will reinforce your authority over the dog.

Frisbee games

Catching a Frisbee and returning it is an exciting game for active, healthy dogs, but it can be physically demanding, and even dangerous, for elderly or overweight animals.

Playing with balls

Catch and drop is a simple game that tests the dog's reactions and obedience. Always throw the ball away from the dog, not towards it. Throwing a ball towards a dog is dangerous, since it could go down the dog's throat when it is caught.

Additional information

Rewarding games

Incorporate training into your games by reinforcing "Come", "Sit", and other commands throughout and by using play as the reward. If other people participate in the games, the dog will learn to enjoy the companionship of all humans.

Using toys

After playing, put the toys away in a box. The dog will learn that the toys belong to you, and that it can only play with them under your terms. This makes the toys more desirable, so that you can use them as rewards during training.

Following a scent

Many dogs, especially scent hounds, enjoy the mental concentration of following a scent trail. Lay down a track for the dog by walking through grass, leaving a reward at the end.

Tug-of-war

Only play tug-of-war when the dog learns to drop an object on command *(see page 94)*, and always use specially made, robust toys. Never play mouth games with possessive dogs, since they might react aggressively.

Jogging

Healthy dogs need plenty of exercise, and training the dog to run to heel with you while you jog is both enjoyable and physically stimulating.

Agility Training

Agility training can be great fun for you and your dog. It gives shy dogs more confidence, teaches pushy dogs to be more careful, and instructs clumsy dogs where their feet are! Any dog, regardless of size, breed, or age, can participate. Training begins once a dog is physically and mentally mature and responds fully to basic obedience control. Agility trainers can provide further advice.

"Over"

Lead by example
Show your dog what you expect it to do. With the short lead in hand, walk over the small jumps yourself. The lead ensures that the jump is unavoidable. When your dog performs this task, make sure your hand leads it over the middle of the hurdles.

Jumping over fences
Your dog will learn to jump over a variety of obstacles. Use your hand to lead the dog over the brush hurdle made from a broom head. Stay alongside your dog, using the command "Over" and leading him "by the nose" with a food lure.

Agility essentials

Teamwork

Initially agility work can appear dangerous to a dog. Reassure it that you are working together as a team. Start easy and at a walking pace. As confidence builds, increase the complexity and speed of exercises.

Collars and leads

Use a short, 30- to 45-cm (12- to 18-in) lead. This is long enough to get hold of, but short enough not to get in your dog's way as it practises. Attach it to a simple flat-buckle collar.

Safety first

Keep all obstacles low initially so there is no undue stress when first negotiating them – no more than half as high again as your dog's shoulders should do it. Never force a dog to negotiate obstacles. Your objective is fun, not fear.

Traction

Avoid slippery floors. Provide foot traction, especially for take-off and landing, with car mats or carpets. Clip away excess hair between your dog's pads and keep the nails short. Wetting your dog's paws also increases traction.

Pause table

Teach your dog to go to the low "pause table" as part of its agility training. Command the dog into the "Down" position and keep it there for ten seconds, then release it. This reinforces your control over the dog.

Owner at the end of the tunnel

While two people hold the tunnel steady, and send the dog through from the rear of the tunnel, you wait the other end and entice if through by calling it and letting it see you. When first training a dog to use a tunnel, initially roll up the slack so your dog can see you.

Additional information

Do it yourself

Garden canes set 60 cm (24 in) apart are ideal for weaving. A 2.5-m (8-ft) board, 50 per cent wider than your dog's forepaws and painted with non-slip paint, can be a "dog walk". An old rubber dustbin with the bottom cut out makes a perfect tunnel.

Competitions

If both you and your dog enjoy amateur agility training, consider joining an agility dog club that has experienced instructors and all the equipment specified by Kennel Club rules.

Co-ordinated training

Ask a friend to help you train your dog. When teaching a dog to walk across a plank, for example, the owner can be on one side of the plank and the helper on the other. This way, the dog is less likely to step off.

Control first

Dogs need to be taught to jump correctly – not just to get over a jump as quickly as possible. It is imperative that you get good basic control of your dog before you start teaching agility.

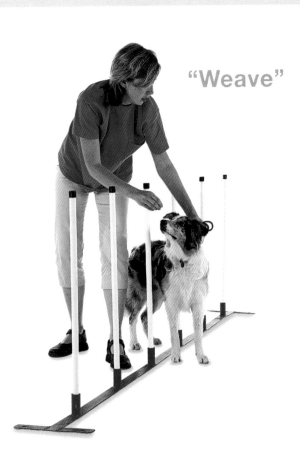

"Weave"

Teaching weaving

With a short lead in your left hand and a food treat in your right, guide your dog's nose through the poles, using hand movement and the command "Weave". This shows your dog what you want it to do. Block entrances between poles with your feet so that your dog has only one natural passage.

Whizzing weaving

When correctly trained, dogs enjoy weaving through poles. However, you should always make sure that the distance between the poles is appropriate not just for your dog's size, but also for its age and flexibility.

Never force

If a dog is frightened or unsure of negotiating an obstacle, lure it over or through, and never drag or force it. Allow the dog to gain its confidence at its own pace, and always reward its progress.

Speed last

Speed should only be introduced when a dog is 100 per cent confident and accurate in negotiating agility obstacles. Speed needs to be tempered with handler control so the dog works the course on the handler's commands.

Hand support

With your right hand under the collar, use your left hand to keep the dog's back legs straight on a beam. If you have an assistant, your helper guides the back legs while you lure your dog forward with a food treat.

"Walk on"

Walking on a beam

Keep your hand in your dog's collar – this keeps its head up and forward, lured by the treat placed just in front of its nose. Make sure you walk it down the centre of the beam.

Training on the A-frame

Once your dog is confident on the beam, move on to a non-slip A-frame. Using the command "Walk on", get the dog to walk up a slightly sloped A-frame. Ensure you train the dog to touch the colour-coded ends of the ramps rather than let it jump off. Gradually raise the angle of the frame.

Catch Games

Catch games are perfectly natural for all dogs, although some individuals are less instinctively drawn to them. However, even a less enthusiastic dog will quickly respond to a series of simple lessons that teach it to pay attention, hold, then catch. Beware: catch games are not jump games. Jumping during catch games is potentially damaging to your dog's joints, ligaments, and mouth.

1 The basis for teaching your dog to catch is basic obedience and fun. Make the catch object desirable by playing with and teasing your dog with it. Train when your dog is mentally alert and keep sessions short. Gain your dog's attention by showing it the desirable, soft, light toy and commanding it to sit.

2 Once you have your dog's attention, teach it to hold the catch toy in its mouth. With both hands, gently roll the toy into your dog's mouth. As you do so, issue the command "Catch". At this early stage your dog is learning to catch directly from your hands.

Additional information

Upping the stakes

As your dog's interest and abilities evolve, increase your distance from the dog. Always use a soft, light toy that is too big to be swallowed accidentally. Never use catch objects that might damage the teeth or injure the mouth.

Variations

Once your dog is adept at catching one toy, add variety by introducing other suitable objects. You will probably have to go back to basics to ensure that your dog finds its new toys as desirable as the old ones.

Praise

Remember to always use vibrant voice and body-language rewards. Dogs are seemingly most proud of their abilities when they receive lavish words of praise from their owners.

Consistent throwing

Your dog can only catch as well as you can throw, so practise your aim until it is consistent. Underarm throwing is usually easier to catch than overarm. Take care not to throw the object unnecessarily high.

3 When your dog willingly accepts the toy directly from you, and does not drop it, progress to the shortest of true catches, only a few centimetres. To avoid your dog dropping the toy, you can make the toy more precious to it by indulging in a short tug-of-war game after each successful catch.

Canine Competitions

Canine competitions range from beauty to working disciplines. Breed showing for pedigree dogs is based on a standard of physical perfection for a particular breed. Working competitions cover an enormous range of activity, from gun dog trials and sight hound racing, to obedience, agility, and working trials. Each activity has levels of accomplishment, often leading to championship status.

Gun dogs

The docile nature and strong retrieving instinct of the gun dog breeds are used in various roles in field trials, be it pointing, flushing, or retrieving birds. Training dogs to work to the gun is best done with a professional gun-dog trainer.

Agility

The agile body and quick mind of the herding breeds make them excel in agility trials. Any dog of any breed or crossbreed can compete in agility. See pages 104–107 for details on how to start teaching fun agility.

Playing with other Dogs

Most adult dogs enjoy playing with other canines if they had the opportunity to do so when they were young. Females will usually play more readily than males, who are more territorial and more prone to fighting. Initial meetings between dogs should take place on neutral territory. Altering your dog's natural body language by stringently tightening the lead can provoke aggression.

Meeting on neutral territory

Arrange for your dog to meet other dogs, with each dog on a lead. Let them investigate each other, but watch for aggressive eye contact. At the first sign of aggression, turn your dog's head away and produce a favourite toy as a distraction. Reward your dog's calm behaviour.

The opposite sex

Fighting is less likely between dogs of different sexes than it is between dogs of the same sex and of similar ages and sizes. Once your dog has successfully met another, whether same sex or not, try allowing them to meet through a garden fence, or in front of your homes.

Additional information

Ownership conflicts

Avoid conflicts over bones and other desirable items by either not giving them at all or by giving them in separate rooms.

Many dogs naturally want what another dog has, even if they have an identical object. Bones and chews are the items most dogs fight over.

Meeting cats

First meetings between a dog and a cat should be supervised. Prevent the cat from running away; this will, in turn, prevent the dog from chasing it.

Responding to commands

Control your dog with verbal and physical commands when it is playing with other dogs. When you are ready to leave, use hand signals and verbal commands to instruct the dog to sit, then go to it and attach the lead.

The same sex

Take care when dogs of the same size and sex meet. You should, however, reward the dog with verbal praise for quietly sniffing and investigating. Take care not to hold the dog on too tight a lead *(see page 137)*.

5

Curing Bad Habits

There is no such thing as a perfect dog. Even the gentlest, most obedient and well-behaved dog can

develop bad habits. Understand why your dog misbehaves and, if possible, remove the cause.

Prevention is always easier than the cure. Clicker training works well but requires extremely

accurate timing on your part. Dogs that destroy homes when they are left alone do so not for

reasons of revenge, but because they are bored, frustrated, or suffering from separation anxiety.

Some habits that we find unpleasant are part of normal dog behaviour, making them difficult to

overcome, but consistent retraining is usually effective. If, however, your dog develops serious bad

habits, seek help from a recommended professional dog trainer.

Understanding Habits

In order to correct bad habits, you must first understand how they developed. You may find some behaviour unacceptable, but to your dog it is a natural way to behave. When a problem develops, work out the reason for it. Ask yourself whether the dog realizes that you regard it as wrong, and ascertain whether the behaviour can be prevented, redirected, or changed – either by yourself or a trainer.

Dog looks content after satisfying its desire to chew

Natural behaviour

Chewing bones, or toys that look like bones, is normal canine behaviour. Chewing a shoe covered in human scent is natural for a dog, but it is unacceptable behaviour to humans. Prevent this bad habit by never giving the dog old shoes to chew. The dog will learn to restrict its chewing to allowable objects.

Destructive behaviour

Although destructive behaviour is satisfying to dogs, it is unacceptable to humans. Giving the dog too many toys teaches it to destroy other items. Limit the toys that you make available to the dog to three or four that are different from other household articles.

Problem solving

Bitter spray

A non-toxic, bitter-tasting spray is available from most veterinary surgeries. In order to deter your dog from chewing inappropriate objects that it finds attractive – your shoes, for example – apply this spray to them.

Confinement

If the dog chews persistently, train it to stay in a crate when it is at home alone *(see page 44)*. Always provide the dog with acceptable toys to chew when it is in its crate, so that it has an outlet for its natural behaviour.

Although a crate may seem unappealing to you, if your dog is crate trained from an early age, it will look upon the crate as its own special den.

"No"

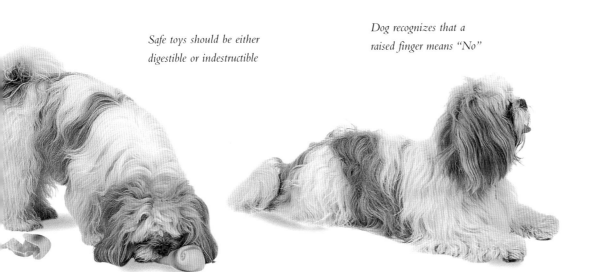

Safe toys should be either digestible or indestructible

Dog recognizes that a raised finger means "No"

Chewing for satisfaction

Chewing is a way for dogs to find out about their environment. Many dogs delight in chewing objects, shredding newspaper, and even peeling wallpaper from walls. However, this desire to be "creative" requires acceptable objects, such as bones to chew.

Discipline

It is important that the dog understands what behaviour is unacceptable. Only discipline the dog when it is actively misbehaving and reprimand it using a stern tone of voice. Discipline the dog as soon as he misbehaves, since later it will not be able to understand the reason behind your anger.

Clicker Training

The basis of clicker training is different from traditional dog training, although food rewards are used in both. Because it reinforces only wanted behaviour, the clicker can be an effective tool in modifying bad habits. When you click, this signals to the dog that its behaviour is correct. A food treat follows, and your dog learns to work out why it has been given the reward.

CLICK

"Mat"

1 Place a mat where you want your dog to go and put a treat on it to act as a lure. As your dog goes to the mat and finds the food, "click" it for being there. Drop another treat on the mat but say nothing. Give no commands. Repeat this, perhaps ten times, until your dog goes to the mat on its own.

2 Once your dog goes to the mat on its own, use the cue word "Mat", without a food lure. Throw the reward near the mat after the click. Your dog learns that the sound of the click indicates correct behaviour and the treat is the reward for thinking properly and responding well. If you click you must reward.

Additional information

Correct clicking

Never use the clicker to get your dog's attention. Its only use is to reward behaviour at the end of an exercise, not in the middle.

Treat follows click

The clicker only has meaning if your dog knows a treat is coming. Even if you click incorrectly, you must still treat your dog.

Quick learners

Be patient and quiet. Allow your dog to think out what you want after you have initially demonstrated what you want. The dog will make mistakes but will learn quickly what behaviour receives a click and a reward.

Watch the calories!

It is best to train when your dog is hungry and use food treats with a graduated appeal, saving the most potent treats for the fastest responses. Adjust daily meals to accommodate this extra calorie intake.

"**Down**"

3 Once the dog is going to the mat, teach it to lie down there. With a treat and a verbal "Down", lure the dog into the down position on the mat. Click and reward. Repeat this several times. Now wait for the dog to go to the mat and lie down without giving the "Down" command. Click and reward.

4 After about ten repetitions, the dog should go down without a verbal "Down". Click when this happens, not before, and throw the treat to the side of the mat. Use the clicker only for wanted behaviour. If the dog does not go down, say "Wrong", turn your back, and try again. Receiving the treat ends the exercise.

Behaviour Interrupters

Dogs concentrate on one thing at a time. I take advantage of that by giving a food treat when I give a dog an injection. The treat interrupts the dog's thoughts of being where it does not want to be. Behaviour interrupters displace the mind from where you do not want it to be, on to something else of your choosing; use them as diversions, not weapons, to capture and channel the dog's energy

Plastic bottle is thrown at hamburger box

"Come"

1 Dogs intuitively respond to sound and movement. A plastic bottle with stones inside can provide an ideal distraction from an unwanted situation. Carry the bottle with you and throw it down it when your dog eyes a "treasure". Commercially available training discs make a unique noise and work well.

2 When your dog is distracted by the sound of the bottle, the unwanted behaviour will be interrupted. Use the command "Come" as soon as the behaviour interrupter lands to call the dog back, then reward it with food, touch, and good words. Soon, the sound of the bottle alone will halt unwanted behaviour.

Problem solving

Environment correction

The dog should not associate the shake bottle or water squirt with you. Pocket the water pistol immediately after use. The effect of the environment correcting the dog is spoilt if the dog sees you carrying out the correction.

Bite sticks

A dog uses its mouth much as we use our hands, to examine things and to fend off activity. If your dog "mouths" while it is being groomed or handled, use a "bite stick" – a piece of dowelling inside a length of rubber hosepipe –

as a safe and effective channel for this natural activity. The bite stick will interrupt unwanted behaviour, displacing it in a direction chosen by you, not your dog, and teaches your dog that biting does not make what you are doing "go away".

Water pistol is fired behind dog's ears

An alternative deterrent

The objective of behaviour interrupters is to be theatrical without harming your dog. Equally important, your dog does not associate you with the interruption. Water pistols are safe, harmless, and effective (especially when squirted behind the ears)

for all but the most water-loving of dogs. A squeezy lemon filled with water also works well. Use it silently, without any commands. When the behaviour has been interrupted, issue a recall and reward the dog's compliance.

Assessing Temperament

It is a fact that dog shelters experience a high return rate because many people choose a dog by appearance, not temperament. Rescued dogs are particularly prone to separation-related problems. If you are acquiring a dog that is over six months old, test it for behavioural problems with a few exercises. Only take on a dog with such problems if you have the time and patience to deal with them.

Nervousness and hand shyness

With the shelter handler holding the dog on a slack lead, quietly approach from the front, keeping eye contact. A nervous dog may bark or cower. Try to stroke the dog under the chin and down its back. Talk to the dog quietly as you do this. A dog that fears hands will pull away.

Fear of strangers

Maintaining control with a slack lead, have the dog examined by a stranger. This will indicate any problems that might appear on visits to the vet or during grooming sessions.

Additional information

Fear of children
Holding the dog on a slack lead, introduce it to a child. The child should avoid direct eye contact with the dog. The dog's response will indicate whether or not it is nervous of children.

Reaction to cars
If you intend to take the dog on car journeys, test its reaction to a five-minute car ride and to being left alone in the car for five minutes.

Reaction to cats
If you have a cat, introduce the dog to it very carefully. For extra safety, put the cat in a cat basket or cage. You should expect the dog to be curious, but a predatory response can indicate potentially serious problems.

Other sensitivities
Some dogs are frightened by loud noises, and others may be scared by unexpected sights, such as umbrellas being put up. Be creative, and test the dog in the everyday situations it will encounter in your home.

Willingness to obey and respond
Take the dog's lead and issue the "Sit" command. From its response you can see whether it has had any obedience training. If it does not obey, try to tuck it into a sit position to gauge its potential for training.

Possessiveness
Holding the dog by its lead, remove its food bowl. Praise the dog, then return the food. If the dog shows no aggression, it is unlikely to be possessive over food. Repeat the procedure with a toy and a bone.

Canine aggression
With the help of the handler, introduce the dog to a confident dog of the same sex. If the dog simply sniffs curiously there should be no problems with aggression towards other dogs.

Pulling on the Lead

Pulling on the lead is the most common problem experienced by dog owners. It can be caused by boredom or excitement, or it may be a manifestation of dominant behaviour. Instead of repeatedly pulling back on the lead, retrain the dog in basic obedience *(see pages 50–55)* and walking to heel *(see page 88)*, and follow the remedial techniques shown here.

The problem

The remedy

Dog strains on the lead

Sometimes the lead itself incites the dog to pull. It is therefore important not to use the lead as an object of force. Do not attempt to match your strength against the dog's. Try to assess why the dog pulls before attempting to correct its behaviour.

Begin to walk with the dog on your left side, holding the lead in both hands. As soon as the dog starts pulling, stop, slide your left hand down the lead and pull back until the dog is in the correct heel position. However, avoid pulling on the lead repeatedly; do it just once, gently but firmly.

Problem solving

No game

Many dogs see walking on a lead as the perfect opportunity to obtain their owner's attention in whatever way they can. Do not let this happen. Instead, you can try distracting your dog or denying it the reward it seeks.

Whatever you do when your dog tries to get your attention, remember not to lose your temper, since then you would be playing the dog's game. This is a time for walking not for playing.

Change of equipment

If the power/weight ratio is very much in the dog's favour, a change of equipment from collar to head collar *(see page 69)* may make controlling the dog's movements easier.

KEY TRAINING

Walking on a Lead   **58**

Sit and Stay   **72**

Walking to Heel   **88**

"Sit"

Hand pulls back once, gently but firmly

Owner gives food as reward

2 When the dog is in the correct heel position, issue the command "Sit". Wait until the dog has done so, then start to walk again, giving the command "Heel". This procedure should be repeated every time the dog pulls forward until it learns to stop pulling on the lead.

3 Once the dog walks quietly and obediently to heel without pulling on the lead, reward it with a food treat. As your dog grows more comfortable with this exercise, you should gradually increase the distance you travel with it to heel, before giving it the food reward.

Problem solving

Stop

Stop walking as soon as the dog's shoulder goes past your leg, irrespective of whether the dog is applying tension on the lead or not. Calmly encourage the dog back to the correct heel position. The dog will soon learn that it gets no reward for being in front of you, and that the only way to get its favourite treat or verbal praise is by walking obediently beside you, with no tension on the lead.

No extending leads

While your dog is learning to walk to heel, do not allow him the privilege of an extending lead. Use of these leads is a major cause of pulling dogs, since dogs quickly learn that by pulling they get more freedom.

No yo-yo

When a dog pulls, most owners automatically let their arms go forward, so the dog thinks that, by pulling, it can get more lead. Avoid this yo-yo routine: keep your arms close to your body and stop as soon as pulling occurs.

The remedies

Lead is kept short

"Wait"

Turning away

When the dog pulls on the lead, use an element of surprise – turn immediately and suddenly in the opposite direction. A short lead will ensure that the dog follows you in the chosen direction. Remember to praise the dog when it follows you.

Hand signals

Whenever your dog lunges forwards, issue the command "Wait" using a stern tone of voice. Reinforce this command by putting your right hand in front of the dog's nose while keeping a firm grip on the lead with your left hand. Release tension before moving off.

Walk backwards

As soon as the dog starts to pull, stop and begin to walk backwards, so you are taking the dog away from where it wants to go. Remain quiet until the dog makes eye contact with you, and is either by your side or following you. When it does, give the dog a treat or verbal reward and begin to walk forward again.

Nice to be near

Make being by your side a good place for your dog. If your pocket contains a food treat or a favourite toy that is given when the dog is next to you and there is no tension on the lead, that is where the dog will want to be.

Don't loom

Think of your body as a tree, not a hairpin. Keep your hands close to your body and your elbows tucked in. Avoid looming over your dog, so your body is not threatening. We want your dog to work to you, rather than you to him.

Titbit keeps dog's attention

No-hand resistance

Keeping the lead attached to the dog's collar, loop it around your waist. Hold the lead lightly and, with your free hand, keep the dog in the heel position by using titbits, a favourite toy, or verbal commands as incentives.

Lead as harness

To increase your control over the dog's movements, you can transform the lead into a harness by wrapping it around the dog's chest. This will also reduce tension on the dog's neck when you bring it back to the heel position *(see page 88)*.

Refusing to Come

Find out why your dog is reluctant to come before going back to recall training *(see page 74)*. Your dog may not have bonded to you; it may be scavenging, or distracted by sexual opportunities; it may have excessive energy or a desire to play. It may also be displaying dominant behaviour, or be afraid of either you or the lead. Never call your dog to something that it sees as unpleasant, such as a bath.

Scent is sprayed below dog's nose

"Ben, come"

Dog ignores owner's calls

Scent obstruction

If the dog is an obsessive sniffer, spray perfume under its nose. This temporarily interferes with the sensitivity of the dog's scenting, so it will not be easily distracted. Scavenging and stealing can be controlled with either a long lead or a muzzle

Disobedience

Dogs can be temporarily distracted by an exciting activity. Vary the play areas you take the dog to, since dogs can be obedient in one location but not in others. Attract the dog's attention by calling its name enthusiastically, then command it to come, rewarding it when it does so.

Extra precautions

Command

Give the command "Come" only when you can enforce it. After thorough recall training at home, graduate to outdoor areas. Work with a long line or an extending lead at first, and take food or toy rewards with you on outdoor trips.

Final rewards

Be enthusiastic when you call the dog, and praise it lavishly when it returns. Vary the end of the exercise period by sometimes commanding the dog to sit, then going to it and putting on its lead. Give it a reward before taking it home.

Lead fear

Never use the lead to discipline the dog, and never chastise it when it returns to you. Do not grab the dog by its collar, since it may think you are playing and try to avoid your grasp. Also, grabbing collars often makes dogs hand-shy.

Sexual distraction

Even if the dog understands your recall command, it might disregard it in favour of a sexual investigation. Neutered dogs are less interested in sex than unneutered ones and more likely to come when called.

Rewarding obedience

Reinforce your recall command by holding the dog by its collar and giving it a food treat. If necessary, use rewards, such as food or a favourite toy, to entice the dog back to you.

Playtime

Allow your dog the pleasure of playing with other dogs, but make sure you always keep an eye on its behaviour. Give the command "Come" if the play starts to become too boisterous.

Chasing Vehicles

The desire to chase is part of normal canine behaviour and its intensity varies from breed to breed, and among individuals. The instinct is stimulated by movement and reinforced if other dogs join in. It is possible to control chasing behaviour, but it can never be totally eliminated. Do not allow your dog to indulge in chasing – it is a difficult problem to overcome and it can endanger its life.

The problem

The remedy

Giving chase

The sight of a cyclist or a speeding car stimulates many dogs to give chase. Because few cyclists or drivers ever stop, the dog is satisfied and considers the chase to be a success.

A wet surprise!

Ask a friend to cycle past the dog. As the dog begins to chase the bicycle, the cyclist should stop suddenly, squirt the dog with a water pistol while it is still giving chase and say firmly "No".

Breed-specific chasing

Lasting stamina

Arctic breeds of dog, such as huskies and other spitzes, are slower than sight hounds, but they have tremendous stamina and are more likely to chase over long distances.

Slow but sure

Scent hounds, such as bloodhounds, and gundogs, like different breeds of pointer, setter, and retriever, for example, are less likely to chase than other breeds.

Built for speed

Sight hounds, of which the greyhound is a classic example, are swift runners. They are also natural chasers, along with herding breeds. Terriers are also instinctive chasers, but they often have short legs and cannot run fast.

Remedial exercise

1 Enlist the help of a friend to cycle past your dog. As the cycle goes past slowly, command the dog to sit, holding a food reward in your hand. Make sure that the dog is under control during the exercise, using a lead or longline; it must not be given the opportunity to chase successfully.

2 Give the dog the food reward for sitting on command as the cyclist passes. Repeat the exercise until the dog reliably obeys your "Sit" command without attempting to chase, even as the speed of the cyclist increases. At the end of the exercise reward the dog with its favourite toy.

Chasing Animals

For thousands of years, dogs survived by chasing and killing other animals. Through selective breeding, humans have diminished this natural canine instinct, but it remains intense in some breeds and individuals, which is a serious problem, especially for livestock owners. If you are in any doubt about your ability to correct this problem, you should seek the advice of a professional dog trainer.

The problem

Dog intently "eyeballs" sheep

Chasing livestock

Unless your dog was socialized with other animal species while young, you should anticipate problems when it meets potential prey. This dog stares intently at a sheep, but it is on a lead and under control. Never allow a dog to walk off the lead on farmland unless you know from previous experience that it does not instinctively chase other animals. You should take similar precautions when it meets any other species for the first time.

Problem solving

Competition

A resident animal may resent a new addition to your home and regard it as competition for food or for your affection. Reduce this risk by feeding both animals at the same time on the opposite sides of a closed door, or by feeding the dog on the ground and the cat at a higher level. Reward the dog with verbal and physical praise when it behaves with curiosity but gentleness with the cat. If the dog is not predatory or dominant towards the cat, the cat will eventually be in control.

Wildlife

One man's vermin is another man's wildlife. Learn the law in your area with regards to common garden animals like squirrels. However destructive they are, they should not become your dog's obsession.

Prey drive

Every dog has a prey drive and most individuals find successful chasing of other species really rewarding. However, this is not to be encouraged, since it is frequently dangerous and against the law.

The remedy

Longline gives owner control

1 The object of this exercise is to channel the dog's chase instinct into a controllable exercise. Experiment with different toys to discover which one the dog finds most exciting. Tease the dog vigorously with the toy.

2 In a quiet and non-distracting location, preferably outdoors, and with the dog on a longline for control, throw the exciting toy, but keep another exciting toy by your side. The dog will instinctively run after the thrown toy.

Problem solving

Seek help

If your dog chases sheep or other farm animals, you may need professional help to stop this behaviour. Sheep chasing is against the law, and the farmer concerned can lawfully destroy your dog since the dog is destroying his livelihood.

Longline

If your dog is an animal chaser, keep it on a longline, so you have control and can get it back from its quarry. Err on the side of caution before letting your dog run free in any area. Successful chases reinforce the dog's natural instinct.

Fright

Many chased wild animals, like deer, are more likely to die of fright than they are of actual wounding or killing by dogs. What may be a wonderful chase to your dog may well be a death run to a deer.

Danger

The dog running after other animals does not consider the crossing of roads in its pursuit. Once the adrenaline starts to run, most chasing dogs simply do not hear your call and often put themselves at considerable risk.

"Jenny come"

3 Before the dog reaches the toy, call its name and give the "Come" command (*see page 74*). Be dramatic when recalling the dog, and wave the second toy to entice it to return. Then play with your dog and praise it.

4 Walk to the thrown toy and pick it up, holding the dog back with the lead. The dog will learn that the toys it chases belong to you. Repeat steps 2 to 4 in progressively more stimulating environments.

Good friends

Dogs and cats enjoy each other's company if they are introduced to each other at an early age. Whenever possible, introduce a dog and a cat when the dog is under 12 weeks of age, and the cat is under seven weeks old.

If either animal is older, allow the resident to sniff the newcomer. First meetings should be supervised, and the dog should be prevented from chasing the cat.

5 Once the dog has been successfully trained not to chase an object of your choice, try a real retrieve exercise in the presence of livestock. Throw the toy in the opposite direction to the other animal, and encourage the dog to fetch it. You will soon be able to control the chase instinct by playing retrieve games.

Aggression with Dogs

Dominant aggression is usually directed towards another dog of the same sex. It is much more of a problem in males than females, and is most likely to take place when the dog is on its own territory. Some dogs are simply unsocialized social misfits, but more often the problem is sex-hormone-related. Neutering at a young age reduces this behaviour in most male dogs.

Signs of Aggression

Barking madly is a preliminary to an at

Eye contact

You should intervene the moment your dog makes eye contact with a potential adversary. A raised tail and intense concentration are indicators that a fight might be about to begin.

A fierce challenge

Dominantly aggressive dogs mean business. On most occasions, fighting is preceded by aggressive body posturing and growling. Unless one of the dogs backs down, a fight will ensue. During a fight, a dog is likely to bite whoever intervenes – even its owner.

Prevention

Anticipate problems

Train your dog to wear a muzzle (see pages 32 and 70). Not only does the muzzle physically prevent the dog from biting, it also diminishes the dog's feeling of dominance. Take a positive attitude to muzzle-wearing – it shows that you are a responsibile owner. Look around you when you are in the park; the safest dog is a muzzled dog!

Professional help

Aggression towards other dogs can sometimes be related to a lack of early and continuing socialization with other dogs. This can be difficult to deal with, and you may need the help of a behavioural expert.

Between you and the dog

Some dogs will aggressively defend their owners. Standing between you and the other dog while pulling on the lead enhances the dog's feeling of aggression. The dog will eventually associate the feeling of straining on a lead with aggression, while it may show no aggression off the lead.

Tight-lead syndrome

Although you may instinctively try to keep the dog on a short lead when aggressive behaviour begins, this will often exacerbate the situation. Forcibly pulling the dog back will increase its aggression. You should turn your dog's head away, so that it cannot make eye contact with the other dog.

Additional Information

Male neutering

Although spaying females is seen as a sensible way to control unwanted pregnancies and behaviour, some people still object to castrating dogs – a far less invasive procedure. Surgically speaking, castration is a minor operation.

The remedies

Dog concentrates on potential reward

Using distraction

When you encounter a potentially aggressive situation, you should attract your dog's attention with its favourite toy, and then issue a "Sit" command. Always reward the dog's good behaviour.

Practising recall training

Starting in a quiet and non-distracting environment, preferably outdoors, practise recall training with the dog *(see page 74)*. Retrain the dog on an extending lead or longline to return to you on command for a favourite toy.

Similar problems

Dogs that are equals are more likely to fight with each other than with dogs of different size, age, or sex. Some breeds – Dobermanns, for example – are more prone to aggression between equals than are other breeds.

Maternal aggression

Female hormones can heighten maternal aggression. During twice-yearly periods of hormonal increase, some dogs become possessive and irritable. Neutering diminishes this form – but not all forms – of female aggression.

Fearful aggression

Many instances of apparent canine aggression are actually examples of defensive, rather than aggressive, behaviour. The dog wants the other dog to go away, not to fight with it. This type of behaviour is usually encountered in dogs that have been inadequately socialized or that have had a bad experience. Professional help may be needed to help socialize the dog so that it can learn to interact with other dogs without resorting to aggression.

A real-life situation

When the dog has been retrained to come to you in a quiet area, practise in the open with another dog in the distance. Reward your dog for not being aggressive. Every day, reduce the distance between the dogs, rewarding your pet for its calm behaviour.

Aggression with People

Most dogs are content to be treated as subordinate members of the pack, and to obey the commands of all members of their human family. Some dogs, however, are unwittingly taught by their owners that they are the real leaders of the pack. Once a dog thinks that it is the pack leader, it might use aggression to enforce its control. You may need a professional dog trainer to correct this behaviour.

Dog's plea for attention is ignored

"Off"

No response
Withdraw all affection from the dog. In order to regain your attention, the dog must do something for you. Disregard the dog until it stops making demands, then command it to sit and stroke it. The dog will quickly learn that you are in control.

No comforts
Give the command "Off" as soon as your dominant dog climbs on to the furniture where you do not want it to be. Make sure that the dog wears a houseline at home, since this reduces the risk of bites and gives you greater control.

Additional information

Open-plan bed

A dominantly aggressive dog should wear a houseline at all times. Ensure that its sleeping area is in the open, and not in an enclosed space. Dogs feel more secure in dens, and a dominant dog's confidence should not be enhanced.

Last to eat

In the wolf pack, the leader eats before his subordinates. Prepare the dog's food, but do not offer it until you have finished eating. Do not give the dog any food treats between meals during the weeks of retraining.

Fetch exercises

Carry out pick-up and retrieve exercises, since these help teach the dog that you are the leader. Make sure that the dog wears a houseline during these exercises.

Medical intervention

Dominant aggression is a potentially serious problem. Consult your vet, who may suggest that retraining will be most effective under medical supervision.

Restrained dog quietly obeys "Sit" command

Last to leave

Do not let the dog charge out of the door in front of you. Leaders go first, and you are the leader of the pack. The dog must adjust its pace to yours.

Frequent grooming

Groom a dominant dog at least once a day, ensuring that its mouth is closed and that it wears a houseline. You should also carry out at least two prolonged lying down sessions *(see page 76)* daily for three weeks.

No risks

Using a muzzle or adjustable head collar *(see page 32)* to ensure that the dog's mouth is closed will subdue the dog, reduce the risk of bites, and encourage it to respond to commands.

Fear Biting

Although the snap of a fearful dog's jaws may look like dominant aggression *(see page 140)*, fear biting has different causes and requires different correction. The fear-biting dog is more apprehensive, and more likely to cower behind its owner's legs, than an aggressive animal. The problem usually results from inadequate socialization in some individuals, but it can be genetic, as in German shepherds.

The problem

The remedy

Fearful aggression

The fear-biting dog often gives out mixed signals. It may cower near its owner and wag its tail submissively, but then lunge forwards provocatively. Dogs with this problem usually have low self-esteem. Asserting your authority during training only exaggerates the dog's lack of confidence.

1 You will need the help of a friend, although a professional trainer can be more useful, and the training should be slow and cautious. The dog should be on a long lead, and should not have been fed before the exercise. Your friend should walk away, holding a food treat.

Problem solving

Canine phobia

The fear of other dogs may result from lack of early experience with other canines or from being overprotected by owners, when young. It could even be a consequence of having previously been frightened or bitten.

The remedy

With the help of a friend who has a placid dog, go for a walk in an open space, and find the distance at which your dog does not show fear in the presence of the other dog. Reward the dog with food treats and affection when it displays relaxed behaviour. Every day, reduce the distance separating the two dogs until your dog walks fearlessly beside the other. Retraining of this kind usually takes three to six weeks.

No challenge

Most fear-biting dogs would rather flee than fight. Taking the ability to flee away from the dog often triggers fear biting, since the dog feels that its life is at stake.

2 Allow the dog to walk towards your friend or trainer and take the food treat from an open palm. Your friend should not speak to the dog, and he should kneel down with his back to it, avoiding all eye contact with the dog.

3 Carry out steps 1 and 2 several times, then repeat them with your friend turning his body slightly towards the dog and still keeping the food treat in an open palm. There should still be no eye contact between your helper and the dog.

Problem solving

Trust

Fear-biting dogs usually have learned from experience not to trust humans. There is no quick route to teaching your dog to trust humans, since it is a process that requires time, patience, and effort. Persevere.

Critical distance

Every animal has an invisible circle around it in which it feels safe. Fear-biting dogs are particularly aware of possible transgression into their safe space.

No reinforcement

If a dog growls at you as you approach, stand still and make no eye contact. Slowly walk backwards until the dog is no longer fearful. Do not reinforce the dog's behaviour by saying "It's okay" – the dog will hear "It's okay to growl".

Body language

By lowering your body posture, you also lower the perception of your threat to a fearful dog.

4 After you have successfully completed the exercise over a period of several days, proceed to the next stage. Repeat steps 1 and 2 with your friend still kneeling down, but this time he should turn to face the dog as he offers the food reward.

5 Walk the dog towards your friend, who should remain stationary. Avoiding eye contact, your friend should face the dog, offer the food treat, and step back. If the dog becomes fearful at this stage, go back to the previous stage and repeat it.

No stare

Avoid eye contact with a fearful dog. Staring into a dog's eyes can be confrontational to a fearful dog.

Slowly

All approaches towards a nervous dog should be quiet and slow. Avoid jerky movements and loud voices. Be prepared to back off until the dog settles.

Smile

Softening your own facial expression should help relax a fearful dog.

Do not loom

Leaning toward a fearful dog can worry it. Allow the dog to come to you in its own time. Reward its new trust with food initially and allow it to learn to like your touching it when it is ready to be touched.

6 Walk towards your friend, and as the dog takes the treat, praise it and stroke it along its body. Your friend should still be avoiding eye contact with the dog, but he can talk quietly to you. It will probably take several weeks to reach this stage.

7 Once the dog behaves confidently while you stroke it and your friend gives it a food treat, he should give the snack while stroking the dog's side. After repeating this exercise many times, make a subtle change. Still avoiding eye contact, your helper should stroke the dog before giving the food reward.

Guarding

Possessiveness is most frequently encountered in dominant dogs. These dogs see themselves as pack leaders and decide that they own toys, food bowls, and resting places. Avoid confrontations with a possessive dog by not giving it toys and not allowing it to sit on your furniture. Treat this problem by withdrawing affection, keeping your dog on a training lead, and reteaching basic commands.

The problem

The remedy

Food bowl only contains rice

Dog watches as owner adds tasty food to its bowl

Guarding food

If your dog growls as you approach its food bowl, try the following exercise. Do not feed the dog before the exercise, and ensure that it is held on a training lead by a responsible adult. Offer the dog a bowl containing a small amount of bland food, such as rice, instead of a full bowl of tasty food.

Whet its appetite

Let the dog sniff the food. With the dog watching, introduce a small amount of tastier food. Repeat this exercise every time you feed the dog and, after several days, it will begin to welcome your visit to its food bowl.

Problem solving

Guarding food
Raising the dog's food bowl on a stool makes it much harder for the dog to stand over and often overcomes a food-guarding problem.

Guarding toys
Toys belong to the owner. A toy-guarding dog is allowed to have toys only to play with the owner, who always wins the game, finally exchanging the toy for a titbit. Put the toy away. Do not play tug-of-war with a toy-guarder.

Owner-possessive
If your dog is possessive of you, keep it on a lead so that you can control it when visitors arrive. Leave a food snack near the front door for a friend to bring in. As the visitor enters, command the dog to sit and stay. Tell the visitor to avoid eye contact with the dog, and to crouch down and offer the snack.

The problem

The remedy

"Off"

Guarding furniture
Dominant dogs choose their resting places. This dog has chosen a chair and is guarding it, along with a toy that it considers its own. You should never pull on a dominant dog's collar, since it may try to bite.

Paws off!
Keep the dog's training lead on throughout the day – this will ensure that you have complete control. Induce the dog to leave the chair by issuing the command "Off" and offering a food reward. A slight jerk on the lead may be necessary at first.

Rivalry between Dogs

Jealousy and rivalry tend to occur in dogs of the same sex, size, age, and temperament. There are also breed predispositions – for example, Dobermanns experience strong sibling rivalry. Dogs cannot share covetable items, so make sure that each dog has its own food bowl and bed. Neutering the underdog may be necessary to increase the difference between two male dogs.

Mutual rewards are given without provoking jealousy

Arguing over possessions

Bones are the objects most likely to provoke arguments between littermates. Avoid potential problems either by not giving bones at all, or by giving them in separate rooms. It does not matter how many bones you offer – one dog will always want the other dog's bone.

Mutual rewards

If the dogs have similar personalities and there are no clear indications that one is dominant, issue joint commands, such as "Sit", and reward both dogs at the same time. They will learn to be obedient in each other's presence.

Jealous of a new puppy

Introducing a puppy

Although most dogs eventually enjoy another dog in the home, there may be some jealousy at first. Give the resident dog plenty of attention in the presence of the new arrival – it will soon associate the puppy with pleasurable activites.

Allow escape

Puppies can be fun, but also exasperating. The resident dog may tire of the constant pestering from the youngster. Set up a barrier so that the older dog can escape from the puppy's demands, or crate train your puppy *(see page 44)*.

Gentle disregard

When the new puppy is absent, ignore the older dog. It will learn to associate the presence of the puppy with increased attention from you.

Mutual enjoyment

Feed the resident dog and the new puppy together, but make sure that there is no eye contact between them. Feed the older dog as often as the puppy, but without increasing the total quantity of its food.

Avoid eye contact

Reduce rivalry by feeding your dogs together, but ensure that they face in opposite directions. Each dog will learn that it will receive a food reward if it eats with the other without fighting. Always put the dominant dog's bowl down first. Always supervise multiple dogs feeding.

Greet the dominant dog first

There is no democracy in the canine world. If the dogs give you indications about which one is top dog, you should acknowledge their relationship by greeting the leader first. This reduces the dominant dog's need to show its authority.

Problems with Sex

The sex-related problems of urine marking, vagrancy, territory guarding, fighting with other dogs, and overprotectiveness occur mostly in male dogs and are easiest to control in neutered animals. Breeding a dog so that it can experience sex may result in excessive sexual behaviour later in the dog's life. Neutering females can increase dominant behaviour in naturally dominant bitches.

The problem

The remedies

Dog clasps rug and thrusts with pelvis

Unexpected water spray diverts dog's attention

Mounting objects
If a dog is frustrated in its attempts to mount dogs and people, it may turn to furry toys, cushions, or rugs. This behaviour is perfectly normal, but it can be damaging to articles and offensive to people.

Using a behavioural interrupter
As the dog thrusts on the rug, command "Off" and squirt it with a water pistol, which most dogs find disconcerting. The dog is probably bored and frustrated – provide it with mental and physical activity.

Isolation and ignoring dog
If the dog tries to mount something or someone, say "No", remove it using the lead, and isolate it for one minute. Isolation is a symbolic gesture and should only be carried out for very short periods of time.

Problem solving

Neutering

If the dog is not to be used for breeding, discuss with your vet the advantages of having it neutered. Neutering does not alter a dog's basic personality; it simply lessens the likelihood of sex-related problems.

Intact dog

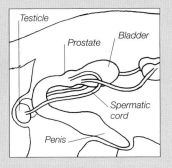

Testicle
Prostate
Bladder
Spermatic cord
Penis

Neutered dog

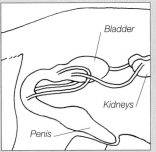

Bladder
Kidneys
Penis

Attention seeking

Inappropriate mounting often starts as experimental and as a way for the dog to seek its owner's attention. It needs action quickly and firmly, because once it becomes learned behaviour it is much harder to correct.

Tug toy is a suitable diversion

Diversion

After one minute, allow the dog back into your company, but ignore it for a few minutes. Then command it to sit, give it a reward, and play with it. Dogs mount objects and people because they need physical and mental stimulation. Make sure that your dog receives enough exercise.

Mounting visitors

Some dogs mount visitors to get attention, others because they know they are not allowed to indulge in the activity with family members. Pull the dog away by its lead, and shut it in another room until your visitor has left. Alternatively, repeat the exercises of isolation, disregard, and command.

Car Manners

Some dogs enjoy car travel, both because they find the journeys exciting and because car trips often end in exercise and meetings with other dogs. Others hate it because of the uncontrolled motion resulting in nausea. Try to take your dog on frequent, short trips so that it becomes accustomed to the car. Reprimand your dog if it shows signs of defending the car as its own territory.

Destructive digging

Left on its own in the car, the dog may dig into and chew the interior. Spray the upholstery and seat belts with a non-toxic, bitter substance *(see page 31)*, and provide the dog with a toy to chew.

Excessive barking

If the dog is unruly in the car and barks excessively, someone should sit with it and command it to be quiet when necessary *(see page 82)*. A muzzle can also help prevent excessive barking.

Additional information

Beginning the journey

Entice the dog into the car with food (if it does not suffer from car sickness) or a toy. Take care, however, not to overexcite the dog before departure, since you want it to be calm during the trip.

Easy clean-up

If your dog dribbles or experiences car sickness, do not feed it before a trip. You may also find it useful to put newspapers or old towels on the seats and floor. This will help to protect the car and make cleaning up easier.

Cars can kill

Never leave the dog unattended in a car in warm weather; even parking in the shade and leaving a window partly open is not a safe option. Dogs have poor control of their body temperatures and can suffer potentially fatal heatstroke as a result of overheating. Even during cold weather, you should not leave the dog alone in a car with the heater on.

A second home

Before setting out, put the dog in the car and provide it with a toy and a bowl of food, so that it associates car travel with enjoyable activities. Remove the food bowl before the journey.

Simple control

Muzzling the dog can prevent destructive behaviour. Tying its lead to the seat-belt anchor will also help by restricting the dog's movements. This can also be achieved with specially designed seat belts that prevent the dog from distracting the driver and reduce the risk of injuries in an accident.

Sunblinds

A sunblind on the car window will help keep the sun off the dog. It can also be useful for calming down excitable dogs, since it obscures their view and makes the ride less stimulating.

Dog guard

Most cars can now be fitted with a grill that keeps the dog securely in its own space. Make the space comfortable for the dog by including a toy to chew and a blanket.

Wait

Practise the "Wait" command so the dog learns not to jump out of the car the moment a door or tailgate is opened. The dog must learn to wait in the car until it is commanded to leave. Start this exercise by getting a friend to hold the dog on the lead in your car, near to the door that is about to be opened. Command the dog to "Wait" and slowly open the door. Reward it for waiting. Issue the "Come" command to allow the dog to exit the car.

Transport crate

Crate-trained dogs can undertake car journeys in a transport crate. In addition to offering safety, a crate will eliminate any destructive activity. The dog will feel secure and relaxed, but you should also provide it with a stimulating toy.

Providing refreshment

Make sure that you have a container of water in the car, especially during long journeys. You should stop every few hours to allow the dog to drink and to relieve itself.

Nervousness

Nervous behaviour is most common in small breeds and in dogs that were isolated when they were young, but it can also occur in many other dogs. Some are frightened by moving objects they do not recognize, such as skateboards or prams, while others fear noises such as fireworks or thunder. Physical abuse may be the reason why a dog is nervous of hands, but equally there may be no such history.

Fear of noises

Make a sound recording of the noise that frightens the dog. Under controlled circumstances, play the recording – quietly at first, and reward the dog for not displaying nervous behaviour. Over several weeks, gradually increase the volume until it is as loud as the noise that the dog is frightened of.

Fear of hands

Place your palm containing a food treat on the ground in front of the dog. If you think the dog could bite, follow the remedy suggested for fear-biting dogs *(see page 142)*. Once the dog consistently and willingly takes the food, reduce the distance between you and the dog, and move to its side.

Problem solving

Submissive behaviour

Very nervous dogs roll over submissively, and even urinate, when faced with frightening situations. If your dog does this during training, you are being too forceful. Get down to the dog's level to restore its confidence. Then entice it to

get up, using a toy. Playing retrieve enables the dog to leave its submissive position without being handled by you, which can make it feel even more submissive. If the dog rolls over when you greet it, ignore it until it calms down.

Hand shy

Nervous dogs want to greet people but are afraid of hands, so they shy away.

The problem

The remedy

Fear of objects

Dogs are sometimes nervous of unfamiliar objects, especially those that move. Dogs that live in families with no young children are often afraid of prams, and they may cower or try to run away when they see one.

Eating near the pram

Place a tasty morsel on the floor near to the pram. Place treats closer and closer to the pram, until the dog puts its head under the pram to eat them. Once the dog is comfortable, place its food bowl under the pram. Move the pram occasionally and reward the dog for showing no fear.

Boredom

Dogs are gregarious social animals, and their senses, minds, and bodies need stimulation. If you return home to scenes of canine destruction, do not assume that it is revenge for being left alone. Dogs are incapable of premeditated crimes against property. Howling, digging, destroying, jumping, and rhythmically pacing back and forth are all signs of anxiety and boredom.

Howling

Wolf cubs howl to attract the attention of their mothers. In the same way, a bored, frustrated, and understimulated dog barks or howls to gain its owner's attention when it is left alone.

Anxious destruction

Dogs can be dramatically destructive, scratching off wallpaper, chewing car interiors, and destroying rugs, clothing, and household linen. This behaviour is most common in underexercised and insecure dogs, especially rescued individuals that are emotionally dependent on their owners

Additional information

Planning ahead

Check the dog's behaviour by leaving it alone in a room, together with a toy. After a few minutes, go back into the room and praise the dog for not showing signs of boredom, such as barking, pacing, or digging at the door.

Repeat this exercise in different rooms and over varying periods of time, until the dog can be left alone without exhibiting any signs of anxiety.

Physical activity

Dogs need physical activity, and the best way to reduce the problems associated with boredom is to give them daily exercise.

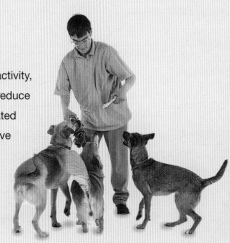

Activity toys

Concentrate a dog's natural curiosity and reward the dog randomly with treats. Fill the toy with the dog's dry food (taking its daily calorie intake into consideration) and the occasional tasty treat. The dog will push the toy around to release the food, occasionally being super-rewarded.

Digging

While some dogs dig to bury bones and others dig to create cool pits to lie in, many do so simply out of frustration. You can constructively redirect your dog's natural instinct to dig in flower beds or on the lawn by providing it with its own sand pit.

Problem solving

Quiet farewell

When you leave the home, always do so quietly. Draw the curtains and leave a television or radio on to mask distracting outdoor noises. Remember that even well-behaved dogs can have separation problems in new homes.

Using the senses

Before leaving, give the dog plenty of mental and physical exercise. Exhausted dogs are less likely to bark, dig, and destroy. Take one of the dog's favourite toys, rub it in your hands to cover it with your scent, and give it to the dog.

Controlled environment

When leaving home, put the dog in its own crate with one of its favourite toys (see page 44). You could also apply a taste deterrent (see page 31) to the areas and objects that the dog regularly chews.

The problem

The remedy

Rhythmic jumping

In a garden, a bored dog may amuse itself by jumping up to look over the fence. Separation anxiety causes some dogs to pace back and forth, urine mark, howl, and dig.

Noisy intervention

String several tin cans on to a rope about 1 metre (3 ft) above the ground and about 30 centimetres (12 inches) from the fence. If the dog jumps and hits the string, the rattling tin cans will give an instant, startling disciplining.

Off to work

Dogs should not be left at home alone all day, since they enjoy activity. Taking the dog to your workplace, if possible, will reduce boredom and minimize destructive behaviour.

Rest follows feeding

Dogs tend to be less active on full stomachs than on empty ones, so they will indulge less in digging behaviour if they have been fed. If the dog is left alone during the day, feed it in the morning rather than in the evening.

Command training

If the dog persistently barks and howls when left alone, train it to respond to the "Quiet" command *(see page 82)*, then set up mock departures. Attract the dog's attention, command it to be quiet, and stand outside the front door. If the dog barks, drop a tin tray or throw a bunch of keys at the door in order to startle it. Return and praise the dog when it is quiet, then leave again. This exercise takes time and patience.

Roadblock

Prevent the dog from jumping up at the garden fence by placing chicken wire on bricks along the base. Make sure that the gauge of the wire is too small for the dog's feet to slip through. The wire will make digging and jumping difficult for the dog.

A helping hand

If you must leave the dog alone for long periods, prevent boredom-related problems from developing by employing a professional dog walker. Alternatively, enlist the services of a friend who can exercise the dog frequently.

Excited Behaviour

Dogs sometimes adopt frenzied behavioural patterns through excitement. They bark hysterically, chase their tails, chew stones, compulsively groom themselves, or demand to be picked up. Consult your vet to ensure that the hysterical behaviour is not caused by a medical condition. With that assurance, you should proceed with basic retraining.

The problem

The remedy

"Sit"

Jumping excitedly

Jumping occurs most frequently when dogs are excited. Homecoming, picking up the dog's lead, or visitors can all stimulate jumping up. Although often an activity of young dogs, this is also seen in understimulated individuals. Frequent exercise can reduce the occurrence of jumping up.

Command obedience

Rather than using a negative command, like "Off", enter the room and give the "Sit" command. Do not raise your voice or wave your arms since both will stimulate the dog. Reward the dog for sitting and stroke it under the chin. Your foot on the lead will prevent the dog from being able to jump up.

Additional information

Meeting children

To reduce the chances of your dog jumping up on children, introduce it to a child under controlled conditions, with the dog on a lead. Instruct the child to keep his or her hands down. Reward the dog for not jumping up.

Begging attention

Some dogs jump up, bark, whine, or lick to attract attention or beg for food. This is canine bad manners and should not be allowed. Never feed the dog from the table. If you give it food, it will continue to demand it.

Forceful control

Always use positive methods to control your dog. Never knee the dog in its chest, step on its hind feet, or squeeze its forepaws when it jumps up. You can control the dog's behaviour with common sense. Be firm, not angry.

KEY TRAINING

Sit and Stay	72
Bark Control	82

The problem

The remedy

"Sit"

Canine missile

While some dogs simply jump up to lick their owner's faces – in the same way a puppy greets its mother – others launch themselves through the air towards people. This is a normal play activity between dogs, but it can be dangerous to people, especially if they have their back to the dog.

Meeting the dog at its own level

You should ignore the dog's flamboyant greeting and, avoiding eye contact, walk past it. When the dog's feet are back on the ground, give the "Sit" command, then get down to its level. Praise the dog's obedience.

Problem solving

Excessive barking

Many dogs act like canine alarms, barking when they hear unexpected noises. Some dogs, however, especially terriers, poodles, and lhasa apsos, become chronically excessive barkers unless they are taught to control their behaviour. The barking often becomes rhythmic, and may only stop momentarily on a command from the owner. To the hysterical dog, your shout of "Quiet" appears to be an attempt to join in.

Voice control

Go back to teaching the "Speak" and "Quiet" commands *(see page 82)*, in controlled situations. Enlist the services of a friend, who can ring the doorbell while you practise the exercise.

Barking

Not all barking is compulsive; most barking is natural. Only uncontrolled or excessive barking is wrong. If this occurs and the dog will not stop, hold it by the scruff of the neck, obtain direct eye contact, and say "Quiet".

Demanding attention

Pick me up!

Insecure dogs sometimes become hysterical if they are not picked up. This is most common in dependent dogs, especially in new environments. The demands become more obsessive if the dog is not picked up, and the behaviour becomes chronic, since the adrenaline released acts as its own reward.

Jack-in-the-box

Some dogs repetitively bounce surprisingly high in the air in an attempt to lick a human face. You should not be domineering with dogs who behave like this because they need to gain more self-esteem.

Licking

Obsessive licking of the forepaws can be a grooming disorder, like obsessive hand washing in humans. It is most common in Labrador retrievers and Dobermanns. Consult your vet, who may want to use drugs to control the activity.

Tail chasing

When highly excited, some dogs, especially bull-terriers, chase their tails. Although there is a strong genetic component to the behaviour, the activity is self-rewarding and increases in frequency unless it is stopped.

The remedy

Divert the tail chaser's attention by offering another reward. Command the dog to sit and, when it obeys, reward it with a chew toy or food snack. You should seek veterinary advice if the problem persists.

The remedy

1   If the dog persistently and obsessively jumps up at you or scratches you with its paw, quietly leave the room. The dog will be surprised at your sudden departure and should calm down.

2   A minute later, and when the dog is calm, return to the room and reassert control over the dog by commanding it to sit. You should always reward the dog's good behaviour.

Food Problems

From the time your dog enters your home, train it to eat only from its own bowl. Feeding the dog after people have eaten helps to teach it to obey commands, since it learns that humans are more dominant than dogs. Do not leave food in accessible places, or feed the dog from the dining table, and make sure that your rubbish bin has a secure lid.

Stealing food

"Leave"

1 If the dog scavenges in the rubbish bin, set up situations that will entice it to carry out a raid in your presence. As soon as you see the dog doing this, firmly give the command "Leave", so that it understands that the activity is not permitted.

2 Put the lid firmly on the bin, then make the rubbish less enticing by spraying the bin with a non-toxic, bitter-tasting substance *(see page 31)*. Let the dog investigate the sprayed bin. For this method to be effective, the unpleasant taste of the bin must be greater than the reward of a raid.

Problem solving

Eating animal droppings

Use standard obedience training to deter your dog from scavenging herbivore droppings. If you see the dog looking with interest at an animal dropping, give the command "No". If it picks it up, give the command "Drop".

Eating dog droppings

Dog droppings can pass on intestinal parasites if eaten and can cause a bacterial overgrowth condition in the intestines, resulting in chronic diarrhoea. To overcome this habit, taint a recently passed stool with Tabasco sauce.

Refusing food

Some dogs refuse to eat their food. This is common among toy breeds, but also occurs in large, lean breeds, such as the saluki. Dogs can go without food for longer than humans. A healthy dog will not starve if food is present. With your vet's approval, offer food for ten minutes, then remove uneaten food. Repeat the exercise daily with smaller amounts, until the food is eaten.

Begging

Begging from the table

Dogs that beg for food from the table can be a real nuisance, and giving an occasional treat is actually worse than responding to the dog every time. Constant habits are easier to alter than occasional occurrences.

1 Train the dog to take food only when permitted. Command it to sit while you prepare its food, and always prepare the dog's food away from the table.

2 Put the food on the floor, but keep the dog in the sit position until you release it with the command "Take it" or "OK".

Fighting Obesity

Overfeeding your dog will shorten its life and may well adversely affect the quality of its life. Consult your vet if you think your dog may be overweight. In most breeds you should be able to easily feel your dog's last ribs, and most breeds should have a perceptible waist. If your dog is overweight, reduce its daily intake of calories and increase its level of activity.

Games with dogs outdoors
Off-lead exercise is real exercise, allowing the dog to be a dog. The amount and complexity of the exercise will vary according to the dog's age, breed, and health.

Exercise through constructive play
Shared games with you, either indoors or outdoors, improve not only your relationship with your dog, but also the quality of your dog's life, since you will be allowing the dog to use both its mind and its body.

Problem solving

The right food

Feeding a good-quality food in the right quantity and sticking to that regime should ensure your dog keeps to the right weight. Human titbits should not form any real part of your dog's diet.

Sad eyes

Do not be blackmailed by the dog who pesters you to feed it on demand or looks at you with sad eyes to share your food with it.

Titbits as rewards

When you are using titbits in training or as a reward, be sure they are quality food, and consider their calories when establishing your dog's overall daily calorie intake.

Exercise through retrieval games

Teaching your dog to retrieve *(see page 93)* opens up a whole new world of shared games. The exercise in retrieving concentrates the dog's mind while at the same time promoting healthy aerobic activity.

Carrying skills

Make good use of your dog's retrieving and carrying ability even when walking on the lead. Most working breeds thrive on doing things, even seemingly uninteresting things like carrying their owner's umbrella.

Effective Training

If you want to be an effective trainer, your dog must respect you and think of you as leader of the pack. If you allow your dog to make decisions on feeding and sleeping, for example, it will soon believe that it is the dominant member of the household. Keeping a record of how you behave with your dog will help you discover whether you have laid the groundwork for effective dog training.

Professional help

Help in training your dog is always available. Contact your local veterinary clinic for details of classes in your area.

Puppy socialization classes

Open to owners and puppies under approximately 16 weeks old, these weekly classes are an ideal method of introducing young dogs to other puppies and to people. Puppy parties should provide a firm foundation for more formal training.

Basic obedience classes

These classes are open to older dogs as well as to puppies that have not attended socialization classes. They are usually held by experienced dog trainers. Their aim is to teach both you and your dog the basics of canine obedience.

Advanced training classes

Although basic training is perfectly adequate for most dogs, advanced training gives you more refined control of your pet. By introducing both you and your dog to the enjoyment of canine agility, tracking, purpose-made activity games, and other dog sports, advanced training helps to develop the full potential of the partnership between you and your canine companion.

Kennel training

Some kennels offer residential training courses for dogs, where your dog is trained in your absence. Although residential training can be useful for specific and specialized work, it is always best if you and your dog are able to train together.

Personal training

Some behavioural problems – for example, certain forms of aggression or livestock chasing – are so serious that they warrant the help of a personal trainer. Your vet should be able to suggest a qualified trainer or behaviourist.

Veterinary help

If you do not plan to breed from your dog, you should consider neutering. Early neutering reduces, or even eliminates, the risk of mammary tumours and womb infection in females, and prostate problems and perianal tumours in males. Neutered dogs also tend to be most responsive to training. If your dog is not behaving normally, or if behavioural problems develop, you should consult your vet. Changed behaviour might be a sign of illness, and in exceptional circumstances your vet may suggest a short course of medication for certain behavioural disorders.

The chart and what it means

Complete the chart

Fill in the chart below (make a photocopy of it first if you don't want to write in the book) with a tick in the appropriate box for each question. When you have finished, see which column contains the most ticks.

How did you score?

If your answers to the questions in the chart are mainly in the first column, you are well on your way to effective dog training. If most of your answers are in the second column, however, you will benefit from some professional advice from an experienced dog trainer.

TRAINING RECORD				
Where did you acquire your dog?	Breeder/Friend		Advertisement/Shelter/Pet shop	
How old was your dog when you acquired it?	Under 26 weeks		Over 26 weeks	
Has your female dog been neutered?	Yes		No	
Has your male dog been neutered?	Yes		No	
Have you previously owned a dog?	Yes		No	
When is your dog fed?	Set times		On demand	
Does your dog eat after you?	Yes		No	
When does your dog relieve itself?	Set times		On demand	
Where does your dog sleep?	Kitchen/Outdoors		Bedroom/On bed	
How often is your dog groomed?	Frequently		Infrequently	
How does your dog react to grooming?	Dog is willing		Dog is unwilling	
When is your dog exercised?	Set times		On demand	
How long is the exercise period?	More than 1 hour per day		Less than 1 hour per day	
Do you have off-lead control?	Yes		No	
Where are the dog's toys kept?	In toy container		On floor	
How often does your dog play with other dogs?	Frequently		Infrequently	
How often does your dog play with other people?	Frequently		Infrequently	
How often is your dog left at home alone?	Frequently		Infrequently	
How often does your dog have special playtime with you?	Frequently		Infrequently	

Index

Acknowledgments

Author's Acknowledgments

By one of those curious quirks of fate that happen every now and then I learned only after Patricia Holden White had been my literary agent for several years that I had been referring difficult dogs to her dog training club. By day Patricia is a literary agent, handling the accounts of authors and illustrators; in the evenings she is one of Great Britain's leading dog trainers. So Pat was the best choice for co-author of this book. We have both been influenced by the logic of sensible, pragmatic, and realistic dog trainers like John Rogerson and the late John Fisher in the UK, and the Monks of New Skete and Terry Ryan in the United States. I am so grateful to Pat for organizing both the human and the dog models for the photo shoots and in ensuring that all performed so efficiently.

Thanks also to the DK team: Deirdre Headon, Lee Griffiths, Wendy Bartlet, Heather Jones and David and Sylvia Tombesi-Walton at Sands Editorial for sorting out the typical, yet always unexpected, little niggles in the book's production with their usual efficiency and grace.

Patricia Holden White would like to thank everyone who contributed their time, help and loan of dogs for both the original and revised editions of this book. In particular, thank you to members of the Hammersmith Dog Training Club, John Uncle and members of his London Canine Training Establishment, Alan Menzies and members of the Alan Menzies Dog Training Club.

The kind and non-confrontational methods used in this book are based on an amalgamation of training philosophies, tried and tested over the years to work for most dogs. The work of John Rogerson, John Holmes, Gail Fisher, Terry Ryan, and Turid Rugaas have played an enormous part in shaping my own dog training methods. Major thanks goes to Roy Hunter whose Anglo-American Dog Training has lit the candle of enlightenment for literally thousands of dog trainers worldwide in the furthering of better, kinder, dog training. I have worked with Bruce Fogle on many Dorling Kindersley books. We have shared and enjoyed looking at dog training from two different but kindred points of view. Thank you, Bruce, for the continued fun and privilege of working with you. And thanks to a brilliant DK team who have brought this project to happy fruition.

Publisher's Acknowledgments

Dorling Kindersley would like to thank the following people for lending dogs and for modelling:

Malcolm and Melissa Ambrose (*Jemima*); Linda Ashton (*Merlin*) Hermione Austin (*Tigger* and *Erasmus*); Gill Bartlett (*Katie*); Jessica Berkeley; Vicky Bickell; Charlotte Bishop (*Floss*); Ian and Rebecca Bowman (*Dottie*); Anna-Marie Brocchi (*Cita and Aila*); Meriel Brook-Withnell (*Platek*); Sheila Butler (*Henry*) Mrs Cardiel (*Dylan*); Pamela Clarke (*Freo*); Suzanne Collins (*Karma* and *Harvey*); Keeley Daines (*Jordan*); Christine Davis (*Spike* and *Thomas*); Mel Dawson (*Digby*); Mrs Fielding (*Benjy*); Bruce Fogle and Julia Foster (*Liberty, Lexington, and Macy*); Sonia Funcheon (*Tessa*); Donald Goddard (*Violet*); Nicholas Goodall; Lisa and Vanian Graham (*Bonnie*); Barbara Greeves; Michael Guest (*Ben*); Thomas, William, and Daniel Hunter. Billie Ingram (*Arthur*); Rosalind Ingram (*Diva*); Thomas Lamonte Johnson; Jeremy Kane (*Polly*); Collette Kase (*Semtex* and *Ginger*); Norma Kerr (*Cassie*); Wendy Kirby and Stephen Fuller (*Cosi* and *Coco*); Jennie Lodge (*Jake*); Danuta Mayer (*Bilbo, Gyp, Sinann, T.B.,* and *Alpha*); Tim Macpherson (*Lolly*) Elizabeth McAllister; Diana Melly (*Joey and Bobby*) John McClenaghan (*Armi*); Alan Menzies; Jan Moore (*Zenobia*); Peter Muswell (*Maisie* and *Prudie*); Marcel and Jane Nassirzadh (*Carlo*); Christopher Netto (*Brewster* and *Tacit*); Ann Marie Donovan O'Neill (*Fionn*); Maria Peploe; Paul and Persephone Pickering; Paolo Pimental (*Islay*); Carol Rasen (*Zoe*) Michael Rasser (*Freddie*); Tim Ridley; Camilla Sampson (*Humphrey* and *Hubert*); Caroline Schroder (*Sprocket*); Scott Simpson (*Jess*); Maureen Solende (*Bailey*); Lena Stenton (*Taz*); Jane Stevenson (*Henry*); Giles Stokoe; William Thompson; Janice Travell; Jennifer Travell; Sandra Turnbull (*Zen*); John Uncle (*Derby, Ziggy, Billie, and Lucca*); Doris and Rachael Urqhart (*Lottie* and *Millie*); Peter Waldman (*Sam*); David Ward and Jenny Berry (*Mr Badger* and *Hattie*); Diana Veale (*Beamish*); Patricia Holden White (*Quince, Rowan, Damson, Heaven, Medlar, and Gage*); Mrs Wilde (*Emmie*); Rebecca Williams; Winnie Westbrook; Mrs Wood (*Leah*); Chrissie Yggmark (*Morgan*).

Dorling Kindersley also wish to thank Steve Cheetham and Pippa Bush of RSPCA for their advice on the text and Pedigree Petfoods for supplying equipment and materials.

Photography

Key: t *top*, b *bottom*, c *centre*, l *left*, r *right*, p *panel* The publisher would like to thank the following for their kind permission to reproduce their photographs:

All photographs by Tim Ridley except for:
Nicholas Goodall 130-131, 165; Anna Hodgson 5, 6cr, 7c, 8-9 12, 39, 52-53 (background), 66, 68, 96, 114; Dave King 14c, 14cr, 15cr, 15cl; Tracy Morgan 14tl, 15cl, 15br, 18, 32tl, 36tl, 42cr, 45tl, 50tl, 82tl, 102tl, 113cr, 154cr, 155cl, 168cr, 169cr, 169cl, 171; David Ward 1, 7cr, 12, 16tl, 17cr, 17tr, 25tr, 40tl, 48, 52-53, 60-61, 63tr, 64-65, 69tl, 70c, 70cl, 70cr, 71cl, 80-81, 84cr, 84tl, 100-101, 105-105, 106-107, 108-109, 111cl, 111cr, 112c, 112tl, 116-117, 118-119, 120-121, 129cl, 129cr, 130tl, 132-133, 134-135, 136tl, 146, 152, 153, 154cl, 158tr, 159cl, 159cr, 167-163, 168tl, 168cl, 170

Bruce Coleman Ltd: Adriano Bacchella 2, 6c. Eyewire: 4l, 5l. 49.. N.H.P.A.: Susanne Danegger 3, 92. Photonica: Tomonori Taniguchi 28. Powerstock Photolibrary/Zefa: 9. RSPCA: David Dalton 111tl; Cheryl A Ertelt 110. Jacket picture Credits: *Front jacket*: Corbis Stock Market: Charles Mann; gettyone stone: Chris Warbey inside flap *Back jacket*: Ardea London Ltd: tl. Powerstock Photolibrary/Zefa: cl. Spine: gettyone stone: Tim Davis

All other images © Dorling Kindersley.
For further information see: www.dkimages.com

Illustrations
Rowan Clifford 151